Miracles
One At A Time

Miracles
One At A Time

Andy Andrews

Books are available at quantity discounts to schools, civic organizations, corporations, and small businesses. For information, please write to:
Marketing Division, Lightning Crown Publishers, Inc.
P.O. Box 17321, Nashville, TN 37217.

Published in Nashville, Tennessee
by Lightning Crown Publishers, Inc.
P.O. Box 17321, Nashville, TN 37217.

Printed in the United States of America.

FIRST EDITION
First Printing: April 2000

ISBN 0-9629620-8-2

Editor: Robert D. Smith
Cover and Book Design: Brian Dominey & Beverly Wallbrech

LIGHTNING CROWN PUBLISHERS, INC.

P.O. Box 17321 • Nashville, TN 37217
1-800-726-2639

This book is dedicated to Joe Lake, Mick Shannon, Marie Osmond, and John Schneider – the founders of Children's Miracle Network.

Your vision provided energy for the dream to begin, but the passion of your hearts made the dream come true.

Table of Contents

I was seven years old, barely keeping pace as my father strode purposefully through the woods, the dry brush crackling under our feet. August was rarely pleasant in the deep South, but this year had been especially hot; especially dry.

Walking the densely forested stand of timber that day, young as I was, I was acutely aware of my father's mood. The month-long drought our area was experiencing had him worried. I watched in silence as he broke dry twigs from seemingly lifeless trees and examined the wilting, dull color of the new growth under them. We hiked through the dust of the parched creek bed, following it to the beaver pond where our family often came for picnics. The pond was nearly empty and the beaver lodge, usually a site of frantic activity, stood abandoned on dry land.

Without warning, the wind shifted. With the change in direction came a rapid increase in velocity and a perceptible drop in temperature. It became cool within a matter of seconds, as the wind, whistling above, threatened to send branches crashing down around us. Lightning and thunder worked the atmosphere almost simultaneously, creating explosions of light and sound that terrified me. My father, his arms wrapped around me tightly, was also afraid...and grateful.

He was grateful for this violent performance of nature and the hope of water that came with it. As the trees bent with the wind and the thunder covered my cries, my father sat down, pulled me into his lap, and said, "Don't worry. You'll be all right. Something good is going to come out of this. Be still. Be patient."

As he comforted me, the rain came. Not with the gentle drops I had seen in the past, but in wild, silver sheets bursting all around us. It wound through the limbs and leaves, over rocks, and deep into the tangled thickets, leaving nothing untouched.

And then, as suddenly as it had begun, it was over. The thunder and lightning and wind and rain were gone, their energy exhausted. It was still again, but even at my young age, I noticed a difference. The forest wasn't just still...it was calm.

With his hands, my father wiped the drops of water from my face. Only my deep sobs betrayed the presence of tears, not raindrops, on my cheeks. Then he smiled, wrung out the front of his shirt, and motioned toward the pond. "It'll fill back up now," he said, "and those beavers will be able to spend the winter here like they'd planned."

We turned in time to see a doe and her fawn drinking from the already flowing creek. The frogs had started their own chorus as we headed for home. "Ah," my father breathed deeply, "everything just smells clean, doesn't it?" And it did. The very air, which only a short time ago had been hot and dirty, now seemed almost sweet. "Let's sit down by this big oak, Son," he said quietly. "I have something to tell you."

I snuggled in beside him, and in very nearly a whisper, he began. "You know," he said, watching me from the corner of his eye, "you weren't the only one scared a little while ago. Those deer were afraid, too. The squirrels huddled together as close as they could get, and what with all the crashes and booms, well, I'm pretty sure the rabbits were worried. But now, something important has happened. The very event that frightened everyone in the forest turned out to be exactly what they needed."

"Do you hear the birds?" I nodded. "Remember how quiet they were before the rain? Now they're hopping around, chirping, drinking from puddles, and feasting on the worms that come out only when the ground is wet. The fish in the pond have more oxygen to breathe and cooler water to swim in. The dust that was on all the plants has been washed away so they are much cleaner for the rabbits and deer to eat. Nobody likes dirty food."

"In fact, Son, all of us are better off now than we were an hour ago. Just because of the storm. What looked like the worst—turned out to be the best. It was a storm of perfection."

• • •

My dad has been gone now for almost two decades, but I can remember that day in the woods as if it happened this morning. Writing this now, I couldn't begin to count the instances I've had reason to recall his words.

As I was working on this collection of letters, I was amazed at the depth of storms encountered by these champions. What was even more amazing, however, was the level of perfection they have attained. These people have invariably taken tragedy and turned it into triumph. They have used their tough times to learn, to become better people, and to inspire others.

There will be many storms in our lives and most will be more terrifying than that day when I was seven years old. As you read these letters, seek the lessons they hold for you.

Special thanks to Polly Y. Andrews, Alejandra McCurley, Isabel Galindo, Jeremiah Shane Ray, Sandi K. Dorff, Max Reed, and Melia Schiwietz for their creative input.

Special acknowledgement to Becky Dominey, Ed Janiszewski, and Lorriane C. Pittard for their expertise and brilliant editing.

My sincere appreciation goes to Scott Burt, Pat Howell, Al and Robin Koop, Machelle Lake, Jenni Noon, and Stewart Park for their invaluable assistance, advice, and help with the letter participants.

Grateful acknowledgements to all the parents that assisted their children by getting their letters to us.

If she could invent a type of food it would be a combination of mayonnaise and bacon on bread and she would call it Baconainse Sandwich.

Allison Blair Williams

Allison wants to be a veterinarian one day. There is a special place in her heart for God's creatures who are sick or hurt. She is now learning to play the drums in school and is on the verge of beating her dad, Tony, in their regular games of scrabble. Allison is also an excellent baker of brownies and a connoisseur of fine pizza!

Allison's letter came to me during a particularly trying day. Maybe I was feeling a little bit sorry for myself when I opened the envelope and read her words. I hope her letter (and the others in this book) affects you like it did me. The problems I thought were so critical just didn't seem to hold as much weight after examining Allison's life and attitude. The last line of her letter takes the wind from the sails of self pity. She writes, "Without Duke and Children's Miracle Network, maybe I would not be such a lucky girl."

Allison Blair Williams

Mr. Andy Andrews
P.O. Box 3709
Gulf Shores, AL 36547

Dear Andy,

My name is Allison and I am twelve years old. Thank you for helping the children with your new book. I would like for all children to be happy and healthy.

I was born different from the other children. I was missing both of my thumbs and the radius bone in my right arm; also my hands were severely clubbed. I was born deaf, and my right outer ear was not formed right.

I underwent eleven corrective surgeries at Duke Children's Hospital. My mom and dad tell me my arms were in casts the whole first year of my life. At four doctors made thumbs for me. It is wonderful to be able to tie my own shoes and button my jeans. There are so many things a person can do with thumbs. Also at four I received a cochlear implant that let me hear for the first time. There was so much to learn about all of the strange and wonderful sounds in the world. My most favorite thing of all is music. Being able to hear gave me the chance to dance, play handbells, sing in choir, be in the band, and most of all learn to talk. I always wanted to talk like my brother Jay and sister Jennifer. I work hard many times a week on my speech and I am grateful to the people that help me.

All of my surgeries were hard and I had a lot of pain. I still hate pain, but it was worth it. The doctors and nurses were very nice and always helped me. They could make me laugh even when I was crying. One thing I learned being in the hospital is that if your IV is in your hand you can't change your gown but if your IV is in your foot you can't change your underwear. It was fun making new friends in the hospital and playing games or coloring together when we didn't feel so bad.

You asked what I have learned as a result of my problems. It is okay to be different. I sometimes wish life was easier but I am happy, have many friends, and a loving family.

I am very grateful to the people at Children's Miracle Network for giving money to Duke so they would know how to help me. I have been lucky and have met many wonderful people who work hard to raise money for Children's Miracle Network. I can tell they really love children. I hope they can help all the children that are born different or get sick or hurt. Without Duke and Children's Miracle Network maybe I would not be such a lucky girl.

Love,

Allison Williams

"It is the greatest of all mistakes to do nothing because you can only do little – Do what you can."

– Sydney Smith

...a totally devoted family man with a heart of gold. It is evident that his mission is to help others and create a wonderful atmosphere for children and all the people who need extra care and love.

Mick Shannon

You have seen the evidence of Mick's work for years though you might not have been aware that he was responsible. After graduating from Brigham Young University in 1973, Mick went to work as an Executive Director for the March of Dimes. It was Mick who created the March of Dimes Telethon. The March of Dimes Walkathon was also a brainchild of his.

In 1983, with Joe Lake, Mick founded Children's Miracle Network. He is currently the President and CEO of CMN and has developed sophisticated marketing relationships with over 110 Fortune 500 companies including Wal-Mart, Hershey, Marriott, Amoco, Johnson & Johnson, Kraft General Foods, the Walt Disney Company, the NFL, and many others.

Mick obviously has a heart for those in need and he has helped fill a gap for many children and their families. His own family is also very important to him. When asked about any hobbies or spare time, Mick smiled and answered, "I have a wife and eight children of our own. They are my hobby and I don't have any spare time!"

Andy Andrews
P.O. Box 3709
Gulf Shores, AL 36547

Dear Andy:

I am blessed with countless memories of very special kids, their families and the quiet courage they exhibited. Thanks to 170 children's hospitals, the 350,000 people who work there and literally millions who support their efforts, most of these kids go on to lead normal healthy lives.

Obviously, not all do. Tragically not all can be saved.

I met a couple whose fourth child was being treated in a newborn intensive care unit. The baby had never left the hospital having received the most intense and sophisticated care available for all four months of its life. Complications too numerous to detail afflicted this baby. Despite the heroic efforts of the doctor and nurses the baby had no chance of survival.

The parents were in a corner of the Newborn Intensive Care Unit agonizing over the decision to let go. Upon hearing I was touring the unit they interrupted their very private moment and asked me over. They explained that after four months it was time to let their precious baby go in peace.

They hugged me and thanked me for Children's Miracle Network and all it does. They shared how grateful they were for caring, compassionate doctors and nurses who had fought to save their baby. They asked me to thank Marie and the Osmonds for all they do for children's hospitals and children in need. They encouraged me to keep up this work to support this very special place that had dominated the last four months of their lives.

We shared some tears, some hugs and prayed together. It was a prayer of thanks for that special baby, that special hospital, and those special care-givers.

I am thankful for whatever we at Children's Miracle Network can do to ease the pain of children and families whenever, and wherever possible.

Thanks Andy.

Sincerely,

Mick Shannon
Co-Founder
President and CEO

FOUNDER OF THE MEREDITH CARROL FOUNDATION/KIDS AGAINST CANCER

...she is not a typical young lady. She is a person with a big heart, a positive mental attitude and driven to educate and make changes. Her initiative to help and take action inspires many and she will make a difference in this world.

Colleen Duffy

It is not often that one sees a person who is fighting a battle of their own come to the rescue of others. That kind of thing generally only happens in the movies. Colleen, however, has ridden to the rescue of a generation of sick children. Knowing that answers must be found to questions about cancer, it's causes and cure, Colleen is not sitting still.

You will be moved (possibly to action) by her letter. Despite her struggle, Colleen is raising funds for research so that other children may be saved. She is also honoring a friend. After reading her words, see if you don't feel, as I did, inspired to help in some way.

Andy Andrews
P. O. Box 2761
Gulf Shores, AL 36547

★ **Colleen Duffy** ★

Dear Andy,

First of all, I just wanted to thank you one more time for inviting me to be apart of this wonderful book; I am extremely flattered and feel that this is a wonderful opportunity for me to share with others the wonderful lessons that I learned from a not so wonderful disease. Cancer is a word that is Associated with death and suffering and this is a well-deserved reputation, but it also has a sunny side, if looked at from the right angle.

During my freshman year of high school, on New Years Eve to be exact, my family and I were told that I had some kind of lymphatic cancer, which turned out to be Hodgkin's Lymphoma. My family and I were distraught by the news, but thankful that my cancer was of the less serious kind. Over the next six months I received 4 courses of chemotherapy and ten days of radiation. My long, strawberry blond hair fell out. I felt nauseous on numerous occasions and I did not have the energy and strength that I once possessed. The cancer also took a toll on me emotionally as one might expect. The confidence that I had always taken for granted slowly faded and self doubt crept into everything I did and said. This probably sounds all too familiar for people who have had to deal with cancer at some point in their life. However, there is a much different side to this story. My situation is a bit unique because my illness was not the first time cancer had influenced my life. Meredith Carroll, my best friend, was diagnosed with habdomyosarcoma while we were in seventh grade. However, due to her determined and unbreakable attitude and spirit, Meredith beat the disease and resumed her normal life style. Then, the summer before our sophomore year, Meredith's cancer came back and this time the disease took her life. Between my illness and Meredith's death, I have come away from these experiences with, what feels like, a wealth of knowledge, about myself, my life, and who I want to be. Although I would not wish cancer on anyone, I would not trade my experience with this disease for the world.

Cancer has taught me the "traditional" things you would expect to hear from any survivor. It has taught me to not take my health for granted; that every day I wake up and my stomach is not nauseous and my body is not weak, to be thankful. It has helped reinforce my belief, that nothing is all good or all bad; sometimes the good might take some serious detective work to find, but it's there! The most important lesson that I have taken away from my experiences with cancer is the importance of action. So many of us, including myself, cry and get upset about all of the horrible things that happen in this world, but more often than not, little is done to actually change these circumstances. What I've realized, through cancer, is that my tears don't mean anything unless I DO something about it…and so I did.

….Continued

With the encouragement and help from my family and friends, I began my voluntary battle against cancer that we chose to call The Meredith Carroll Foundation/Kids Against Cancer. This foundation was started my sophomore year of high school and has continued ever since. We sell T-shirts at high schools and jr. highs in Illinois. The foundation has 3 basic objectives: 1) to raise money for pediatric cancer research 2) to get kids involved in this process as a form of philanthropy and 3) to keep Meredith's wonderful spirit and attitude alive. Over the past three years we have donated $48,000 to Children's Memorial Hospital in downtown Chicago to support their ongoing research of childhood cancers. This year we will also be making a substantial donation although the total is not yet own.

So as you can see Andy, even something as awful and dreaded as cancer can have a "happy" and positive outcome! Although I don't feel that any outcome can "make up" for Meredith's death, this foundation and all of the life lessons that have come from it, definitely have helped ease the pain and encouraged understanding. These experiences, without a doubt, have played a vital role in the shaping of my personality and attitude, and I would not be anywhere near the person I am today without having gone through these experiences. I can say, with 100% certainty, that these experiences have made me a much more thankful, happy and optimistic person. One cannot always control what happens in one's life, but one can ALWAYS control one's attitude. As Chuck Swindol so eloquently puts, "Life is 10% what happens to you, and 90% how you react to it". YOU are in control of your life.

Once again, thank you so much for giving me this incredible opportunity to be a part of something so wonderful and healing. I wish you the best of luck Andy....

Sincerely,

Colleen Duffy

"An opal lay in the case, cold and lusterless. It was held a few moments in a warm hand, where it gleamed and glowed with all the beauty of the rainbow. All about us are human lives of children or of older persons, which seem cold and unbeautiful, without spiritual radiance or gleams of indwelling light, which tell of immortality. Yet they need only the touch of a warm human hand, the pressure of love, to bring out in them the brightness of the spiritual beauty that is hidden in them."

– J.R. Miller D.D.

...she has earned many awards and honors throughout her career. She is an international celebrity and savvy businesswoman. She is involved in many activities throughout the world aimed at helping others.

Marie Osmond

Marie was only three years old when she made her show business debut on television's "Andy William's Show with her singing brothers, The Osmonds. When she was just thirteen, her first record, *Paper Roses*, reached number one on the charts, and at the age of fourteen, Marie and her brother Donny starred in the top-rated "The Donny and Marie Show" for ABC. Hit records, movies, and major awards have also been her constant companions as an adult.

I became acquainted with Marie personally while working with her several years ago and am always anxious to tell people about the "real" Marie. Understandably, most people think of Marie as a star, a true member of show business royalty, but it only takes a small amount of time to see that she is first and foremost a devoted mother and loyal crusader. Marie truly loves children...hers and yours. She has devoted a large part of her life to making a better world for all of them.

MARIE, INC.

Mr. Andy Andrews
P.O. Box 3709
Gulf Shores, AL 36547

Dear Andy:

Thank you so much for inviting me to share one of many experiences I have had with Miracle Kids through my 17 year career with The Children's Miracle Network.

As you know, I feel blessed to have been one of the co-founders of CMN, along with my family and my good friends John Schneider, Mick Shannon and Joseph Lake. Back in 1982, we conceived the idea of a fund raising organization where we could help the most kids each year (14,000,000 million kids are treated by the 170 CMN affiliated hospitals annually), and where 100% of the money raised in each community would stay in that area to help the kids who are treated by the local CMN Children's hospital.

These kids are the "Miracles", and they are the Champions we all work so hard to help each year. But I have found that behind every "Miracle Child", there is a "Miracle Mom and Dad". Let me tell you about a Mom I had the privilege to meet.

I remember visiting one of our CMN hospitals. I was told when I arrived that we would have about an hour to tour the hospital, see the kids and the staff, and to allow the hospital to showcase the great new equipment that CMN had helped the hospital obtain. Following the tour we were going to lunch in the board room where, for the first time in many months, the entire board and administration of the hospital would be in attendance.

Near the end of the tour, as I walked by a play room, I saw a little 3 year-old girl sitting on the floor playing with some toys, and sitting at the child's table was a very young mom crying her heart out. As the group of us were moving toward

3325 NORTH UNIVERSITY AVENUE, SUITE 150 PROVO UTAH 84604 (801) 373-3600 FAX: (801) 373-3699

11

the next room to visit, I felt I should go into the play room where this young mother was so upset.

I asked Joe Lake to continue on the tour with the rest of the group and I would catch up with them in a minute. As I went into the room, the mom looked up at me and I could tell she recognized me. At that moment she started to cry all the more. As I walked to her, she stood up and without a word put her arms around me and hugged me beyond belief.

We sat down for what would be a three hour visit. Joe Lake came back to get me in a few minutes and I told him that I could not leave this mom right now. Joe explained to the group giving the tour that I would catch up at the board room. This was a very special experience for me, to know a very special mom, whom I shall never forget.

Through the years, I have learned so much about the miracles that are an every day occurrence at these great hospitals, but I have also learned that as good as these hospitals are, there are still some things that cannot be "fixed".

This young mother had just been told that her beautiful 3 year-old daughter had an inoperable brain tumor, and that she only had a few weeks to live. She didn't know what to do, what to say or where to turn, and you could see the heart-wrenching, utter despair. I'll never forget the desperate, yet blank look in her eyes, knowing her sweet, innocent child would soon be gone.

As one mother to another, I was just grateful to be there for her in some way. I'll always remember our conversation and those moments we shared. I'm forever grateful my eyes caught hers and we were able to share a few hours of tears, hugs and love. I missed the board meeting, but I came away with an increased awareness that we have so much more to do for kids and so little time, in some cases, to do it.

CMN Champions and I are totally committed to continue our efforts to help hospitals help kids. The more we can do, the fewer moms, like my new friend, will have to hear the devastating news this mother heard on that tragic day.

Thank God for kids and thank God for all these great CMN Children's hospitals. They are truly making miracles one family at a time.

Much Love,

Marie Osmond
Co-Founder / CMN Champions

"The future belongs to those who believe in the beauty of their dreams."

– Eleanor Roosevelt

Craig, Tammy, Brittany and Holly

TEACHER/DEACON

...they like to spend their time with their family and their church. They enjoy taking short trips and watching their young girls grow up and enjoy their childhood.

Tammy and Craig Rogers

Craig and Tammy live with their two beautiful daughters in East Tennessee. Craig is a Senior Specialist in Information Services for Wellmont Health System in Kingsport where he has worked for the last fourteen years. Cindy, on the other hand, really works! She is not only a full time mom, but a full time teacher as well. Both girls are home schooled by their mother, a situation that, the family agrees, is working out beautifully.

Craig enjoys golf. Cindy likes to shop. She says, "Craig is trying to teach Brittany golf so that she can win the LPGA when she grows up and he can caddy for her. Holly and I like to spend the money they think they are going to win!"

Mr. Andy Andrews
P.O. Box 3709
Gulf Shores, AL 36547

Dear Andy,

Thank you for giving us the opportunity to share our story with you. We know how much it means for us to be able to read how others have overcome adversity and received blessings from their storms. Hopefully, someone can receive a similar blessing from our story.

Our family consists of myself, my husband, and two beautiful little girls, Brittany and Holly. We live in a beautiful area in East Tennessee in a comfortable home near our families and church. Four years ago, life seemed so good, you could never have convinced us that anything bad could ever have happened to any of us. Yes, we had heard of families involved in different kinds of accidents and catastrophes, but still we thought, "That could never happen to us." Little did we know that on May 23, 1995, God would allow a storm in our lives that would change us forever.

I suppose we need to share with you a little about our oldest daughter, Brittany. We feel Brittany was special from the start. She was born on June 20, 1992, five weeks premature, but healthy from the beginning. From the day she was born, people always complimented us on her beauty and friendly disposition. She has never seen a stranger. She is an outgoing child, very active in church, loves to play with her little sister, and just loves life.

On May 23, 1995, Brittany was involved in an accident with a riding lawn mower that resulted in severe injuries to her right leg. We were having a fun afternoon playing in the driveway, while her Daddy was mowing the lawn. Earlier, we had found a nest of baby bunnies in some of the shrubbery in the front yard. Brittany wanted to look at the bunnies again, I knew her Daddy was on the other end of the yard, so I gave her permission to see them again. Instead of looking at the bunnies, she decided she needed to tell her Daddy something, and she ran up behind him on the other end of the yard. He, not knowing that she was there, backed up and ran over her right leg. The sound we heard was just too hard to explain. I had her five-month-old baby sister in my arms and looked up and saw him running with her towards me. She was not even crying. We immediately called 911 and I began to pray to God for Him to take care of her and not let her hurt. He answered my prayers! Brittany never cried at all, in fact, she sang "Jesus Loves Me" in the ambulance, all the way to the hospital.

When we arrived at the hospital, they began cleaning her leg and bandaging it. Her right leg was injured with partial amputation to her right foot and soft tissue damage on the remainder of her leg. The decision was made that it would be best if she were transferred to East Tennessee Children's Hospital in Knoxville, which was about 1 ½ hours away. They would be better prepared to deal with her type of injuries. Putting Brittany on that helicopter by herself was the hardest thing, at that time, we had ever done. But our church family and friends were there offering their support and prayers, which meant so much to us. When she arrived in Knoxville, she immediately went to her first surgery. Her doctors came out and began to prepare us for what was going to be the longest and hardest battles that any of us had ever faced in our lives. At that point, they really weren't sure whether they would be able to save her foot or even her leg.

Of course we had not even thought about arrangements for a place to stay, but the Lord had everything planned for us. The Ronald McDonald House was full and the hotel that usually accommodates families was full because of a convention in the area. There were not many rooms

4821 Lake Park Ct • **Tammy Rogers** • Kingsport, TN 37664

available anywhere. We were given a one-bedroom apartment at the Fort Sanders Fellowship House, about one block from the Children's Hospital, where for six weeks our families would live. It was truly an answered prayer, the first of many we would receive during this storm. We cannot begin to tell you how wonderful and compassionate the people were. The news of Brittany's accident spread quickly. We received mail and letters of encouragement from families all over the area. It was truly a comfort to know that so many people were remembering our baby in prayer. Brittany's grandmother shared Psalm 121 with us and it affirms that all-true help comes from the Lord. God watches over the believer all the time, in every circumstance, and forever.

Over the next few weeks there were many more ups and downs. She underwent many surgeries, or "trips to the Big White Room", skin grafts, life threatening infections, and days on the respirator. Muscle was taken from her back and transplanted to her foot so she would have a platform on which to walk. That surgery alone took more than eight hours. Immediately after that surgery, it was decided to keep her unconscious for several days to give her time to begin healing. After four days, they decided to take her off the respirator and let her regain consciousness. She was off the respirator for a few hours and then we were faced with another apparent storm. She developed pulmonary edema and could not breathe on her own. She had to be placed back on the respirator and we were devastated. Once again, God knew better than we did because for the next four days, she healed more than any other time during this ordeal. At the end of those four days, she came off the respirator with no problems.

She was still having high fevers, but the blood cultures were coming back good. They told us that a lawn mower accident is considered to be one of the dirtiest types of accidents you can have. Bone and tissue were exposed to the soil with the many fungus and bacteria. She cultured organisms that were not even in medical books. They were not sure how long some of the bacteria could lay dormant.

Another family at the hospital shared II Corinthians 1:3-4 with us that tells us of the comfort we have in God. I also found a lot of comfort in the chapel at the hospital. It had a sign that read "Reach up as far as you can and God will reach down the rest of the way." There was also a sculpture hanging on the wall of the chapel. It was of rain falling down, but through the rain, you could see the sun. I came to realize then, that, God was going to bring us through the rain, and the sun would definitely shine again. I began to really thank our good Lord for all He had done for us, and for all that He was going to do for her. I came to real understanding that He truly loves her more than we could ever love her, and that she was a gift from Him. She had only been loaned to us for a while here on earth and I could honestly thank Him for our precious gift. It's amazing the things that you can think of during the long hours of waiting in a hospital room. If I hadn't had God to lean on during this time, well, I just can't imagine what I would have done. All the love and support you have from your family and friends is nothing compared to the love and support you can receive from God if you just trust in Him.

After it was decided that all was going well, and the muscle transplant was successful, the doctors began to explain that many of her growth plates had been affected by the accident. They were not sure as to how well her right leg would grow, if it would grow at all. But as of today, it is actually one half inches longer than her left leg and is doing great. She had spent 18 days in the intensive care unit. Brittany was a true fighter. She spent a total of six weeks at Children's Hospital, and even spent her 3rd birthday in the hospital. But on July 2, 1995, we were able to bring her home.

She has had two additional surgeries to her leg. She had to have a muscle flap transplanted to cover her kneecap. Additional skin grafts were needed for this. And then, in September 1995, she was to begin tissue expanders to her thigh in hopes to remove some of her scar tissue. They were going to release her heel cord at this time also. Her heel was more involved than they had anticipated, so the decision was made to wait on the expanders. This surgery was truly trying on her. She had a pin through the bottom of her heel and she was unable to walk for three weeks. I have a true compassion for people who deal with a wheelchair on a daily basis. She then wore a cast for an additional nine weeks.

She has made lots of progress since returning home. She began physical therapy and much to our surprise, really enjoyed it She has had a prosthesis made for her foot and is now running and jumping, and doing all the things that a 6 ½ year old little girl can do. She goes to gymnastics once a week and barely walks with a limp. She was able to represent the state of Tennessee as a Champion in the 1996 Children's Miracle Network. While doing this, she met President and Mrs. Clinton and then traveled to Disney World and met all of her Disney favorites. She also made many new friends from across the country that had stories similar to hers and was able to share with them how God has truly made her better. We all still pray for her new friends.

The past three and a half years have been full of many heartaches and blessings. We praise God and thank Him continually for providing for us during these times. We cannot pretend to understand everything that has happened in our lives, but we can say that God is faithful and He does provide for our every need. He works in ways we do not understand, but we must know His way is always the best way. If you truly want to see a miracle, you need look no further. We are so proud of her. To God be the glory.

Blessings,

Craig & Tammy Rogers

Craig & Tammy Rogers

...she claims she is an average 7 year old, but if she were an explorer she would explore the ocean in a submarine and would take her sister Holly.

Brittany Rogers

Brittany recently helped her mom redecorate her room in coral, purple, and yellow. She says it looks more "big girlish" now. She spends a large part of her days running, jumping, and doing all the things that girls her age like to do. Brittany loves to have friends over to play and swim. She enjoys riding her bicycle and is especially devoted to her dog, Brandy, her hamster, Sonny, and fish, Mickey.

I asked Brittany what her favorite games were. She answered Monopoly and Uno and then volunteered that she likes to win! This is not surprising because her parents have instilled in her an attitude of winning. Brittany is a charmer who will accomplish whatever she wants as an adult. She has obviously been infused with a wonderful level of self-confidence and a great degree of personal certainty. She has goal setting down, too. I asked, "Brittany, if you could have anything you wished for, what would it be?" She answered, "A swimming pool with a diving board and slide." "If you got that," I continued, "what would you wish for next?" Brittany smiled that big smile and said simply, "A bigger pool!"

18

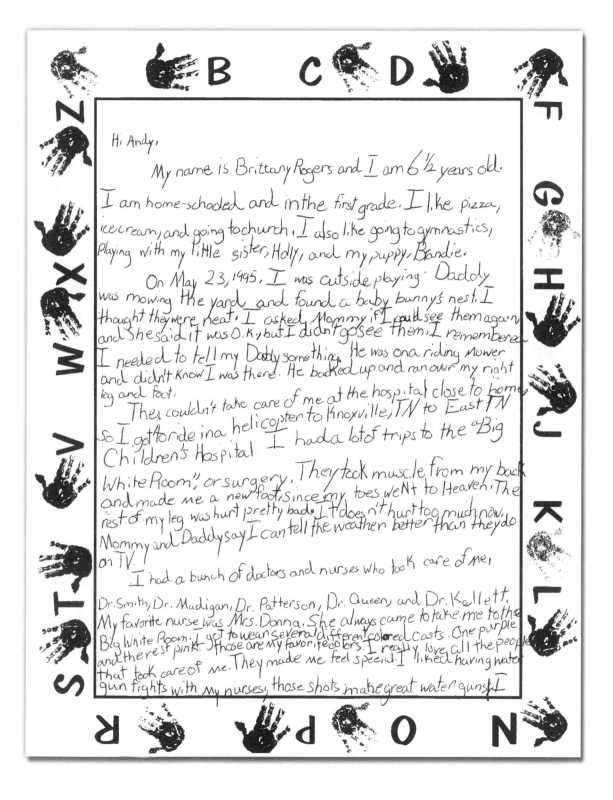

Hi Andy,

My name is Brittany Rogers and I am 6½ years old.

I am home-schooled and in the first grade. I like pizza, ice cream, and going to church. I also like going to gymnastics, playing with my little sister, Holly, and my puppy, Bandie.

On May 23, 1995, I was outside playing. Daddy was mowing the yard and found a baby bunny's nest. I thought they were neat. I asked Mommy if I could see them again and she said it was O.K., but I didn't go see them. I remembered I needed to tell my Daddy something. He was on a riding mower and didn't know I was there. He backed up and ran over my right leg and foot.

They couldn't take care of me at the hospital close to home so I got to ride in a helicopter to Knoxville, TN to East TN Children's Hospital. I had a lot of trips to the "Big White Room", or surgery. They took muscle from my back and made me a new foot, since my toes went to Heaven. The rest of my leg was hurt pretty bad. It doesn't hurt too much now. Mommy and Daddy say I can tell the weather better than they do on TV.

I had a bunch of doctors and nurses who took care of me, Dr. Smith, Dr. Madigan, Dr. Patterson, Dr. Queen, and Dr. Kollett. My favorite nurse was Mrs. Donna. She always came to take me to the Big White Room. I got to wear several different colored casts. One purple and the rest pink. Those are my favorite colors. I really love all the people that took care of me. They made me feel special. I liked having water gun fights with my nurses, those shots make great water guns! I

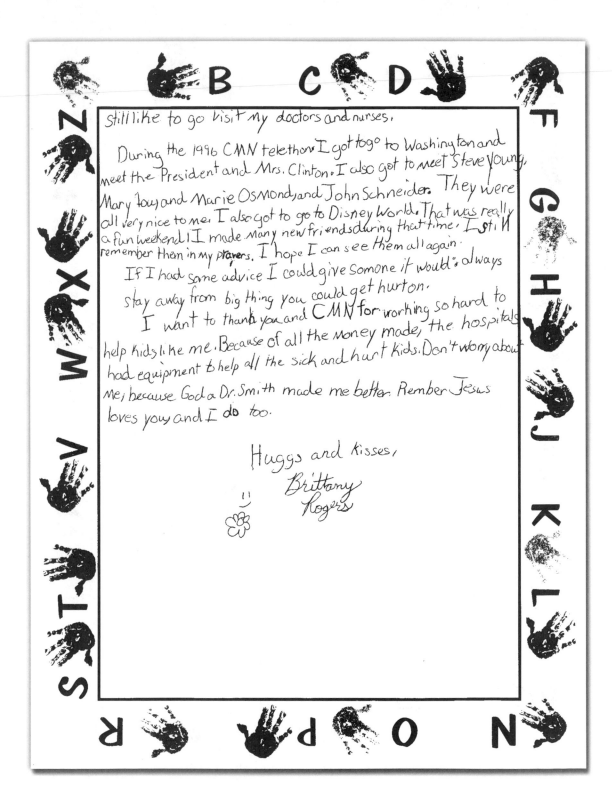

still like to go visit my doctors and nurses.

During the 1996 CMN telethon I got to go to Washington and meet the President and Mrs. Clinton. I also got to meet Steve Young, Mary Lou and Marie Osmond, and John Schneider. They were all very nice to me. I also got to go to Disney World. That was really a fun weekend! I made many new friends during that time. I still remember them in my prayers. I hope I can see them all again.

If I had some advice I could give somone it would, always stay away from big thing you could get hurt on.

I want to thank you and CMN for working so hard to help kids like me. Because of all the money made, the hospitals had equipment to help all the sick and hurt kids. Don't worry about me, because God a Dr. Smith made me better. Rember Jesus loves you, and I do too.

Huggs and kisses,
Brittany
Rogers

"Have I not commanded you? Be strong and courageous! Do not tremble or be dismayed, for the Lord your God is with you wherever you go."

– Joshua 1:9

NEUROLOGIST

...her favorite hobbies include arts, crafts, film, poetry, reading and travel. Her life is also filled with educating people in making them aware of other alternative before surgery.

Dr. Monique Gingold

Dr. Gingold is someone who has used her education and talents in ways that far exceed the public's normal expectations. She truly cares about people, children in particular. Before entering medicine, Dr. Gingold was a pediatric physical therapist. Seeing many exciting changes occurring in the treatment of children with spasticity and cerebral palsy, she decided to broaden her education. Dr. Gingold has also broadened her impact in the lives of many families.

She is now a board certified Neurologist with Special Qualifications in Child Neurology. Her spare time is spent studying languages (she speaks four), gardening, hiking, and photography. "There are many options now available to help children with spasticity and cerebral palsy before rushing them off to surgery," the doctor says. "I hope to be able to share these with any interested parents."

Dr. Monique Gingold

Andy Andrews
P. O. Box 2761
Gulf Shores, AL 36547

Dear Andy,

This is a story in progress. I relay it with mixed emotions and hope that I will one day cross paths with this family again and learn of wonderful news.

Some time ago, an American father entered my office with his beautiful 15 month old Korean-American daughter. The father was guarded and quiet; I found out that she had been born prematurely and, as is sometimes the case, had cerebral palsy which preventing her from walking properly. My initial reaction was to gently question the non communicative father and ask why the baby had not received earlier treatment. Early treatment can often correct or greatly improve this problem and is available free in Federally mandated programs. He avoided answering by saying the military moved him often, the insurance wouldn't cover many things, and the family couldn't afford to pay for treatment, etc. I noticed the little girl would not talk to anyone but would occasionally whisper to her father. After this initial visit, they literally disappeared. I searched through records they had left and began calling home and the father's place of employment. I called, leaving message after message but, the father never returned my calls and the mother never surfaced.

After years had passed, I happened to see the family in the grocery store. I was excited about the opportunity but crushed when I saw they were deliberately avoiding my attempts to catch their attention. I hurried through the line and into the parking lot to find them. As I approached their car, they turned away from me and sped off. I was both baffled and angry, and most of all, hurt for the little girl. It was heartbreaking to know that there was an operation that could be performed that could probably help her.

A fortunate turn of events then occurred. The father sent some papers for me to complete in order to facilitate the family's return to Korea. I took a chance and told my assistant I would not sign these documents until they came in - father, mother, and child - for a re-evaluation and to discuss my recommendations. Only the father and child came. I spoke frankly and told him how it pained me to see his daughter the way she was, knowing how she could be helped with surgery and therapy. I told him that if she were my daughter,I would not hesitate to have her undergo this surgery. He left saying he would discuss the matter with his wife. I was exhilarated the next day when the father called asking if I could help arrange for the surgery as soon as possible! The surgery date was set and time was allotted for rehabilitation. The operation at the base of her spine to relieve spastic muscles was a success. During the course of the rehabilitation, I finally met the mother. I found she was profoundly depressed and had daily crying spells, locking herself in the bathroom. She felt it was her duty to guard her daughter from the world. I now had an explanation as to why this beautiful child never spoke to anyone outside of her immediate family. Unfortunately, due to the family's return to Korea, the rehabilitation stay was cut short.

I only hope that this precious child continues her physical and emotional rehabilitation in Korea, and that her mother, being close to her family, is able to heal emotionally, too. The fact that the operation was performed through perseverance and was successful is a bittersweet victory. My hope is that the entire family is healed. The mother felt alone in this new culture and when she experienced ignorant people reacting with fear to her daughter's unusual way of walking, she tried to do her best, alone, by sheltering her child. From the position of doctor, we can only do what families will allow us to do. We must persevere to educate people to be understanding, supportive, and tolerant of others. We are all created differently. We need to work together, unhampered by fears, prejudices, and ignorance, so that people like my little patient can soar and reach their full potential.

Sincerely,

Dr. Monique Gingold
Pediatric Neurologist

"When you get into a tight place and everything goes against you, till it seems as though you could not hold on a minute longer, never give up then, for that is just the place and time that the tide will turn."

– Harriet Beecher Stove

FUTURE EXPLORER

...wants to be a Jedi because they are his favorite good guys. He enjoys chess and reading. He would like to explore outer space and time travel back to WWII to learn more about Pearl Harbor.

Peter Beal

Peter's hobby is model rockets. He experiments with different engines and sizes and could quite possibly become the first teenager to put a cardboard tube into lower earth orbit. This fascination with space travel has made Peter an expert on all things Star Wars. He is also a big fan of the Star Trek television series.

On earth, Peter is an accomplished golfer and dreams of one day playing on the PGA Tour. He occasionally beats his father in chess and enjoys the music of the group, Jars of Clay. Peter's letter is straightforward. It is refreshing and remarkable for the sense of gratefulness he exudes.

Peter Beal

Dear Andy,

Probably the most important thing I learned from my accident was how God answers prayer and helps us through tough times, and always wear a helmet when you ride a bike. The police, paramedics, and trauma doctors all said I would not have made it if I hadn't been wearing my helmet. All my other injuries were fixable, but the helmet saved me from certain death or serious permanent head injuries.

Because of my Christian faith, I experienced many miracles during the time of the accident. One of the night-duty nurses remarked to my mom that normally kids with the kind of injuries I had would be screaming in pain but she felt such a strong presence of peace in my room. We believe it was because there was so much prayer going up for me. I am thankful for all our church family and friends that came to the hospital and prayed in the trauma unit the day I was hit by a car. There were so many people there that day that one of the nurses asked if I was a celebrity!! Their prayers helped me to recover.

I saw how God uses *people* to work His miracles: firemen, paramedics, the helicopter pilot that flew me to the trauma unit, and all the surgeons and nurses. I am so thankful for the doctors and nurses who worked on me and who dedicate their lives everyday to helping kids. They were all part of the miracle. Now I want to grow up and be a miracle in someone else's life.

I also learned that we *can* get through the tough things in life. The worst part of the accident for me was 9 months of physical therapy and all the pain involved in the healing process. I have to admit I didn't always have a great attitude about it either. I had an external fixator on my femur (thigh) for three months; it was really difficult to move my leg at all because my knee stayed swollen for almost a year.

The physical therapy was very painful. There were so many times I wanted to just give up (I must have said "Can we please just not *do* this?!" a million times), but my physical therapist said if I didn't do it, the joints would stiffen up and I would never walk or run like a normal kid. Plus, my mom and dad wouldn't let me give up; they were always cheering me on, saying "you can do it!"

My life has changed drastically since the accident. We never dreamed things would happen the way they did. "All things work together for good to those who love the Lord and are called according to His purpose," (Romans 8:28) really is true.

After my accident, I just wanted to get over it and get on with my life. So you can imagine how surprised we all were when Children's Hospital called saying I had been selected to be a *Johnson & Johnson* "Safe Kid". Eight months after the accident they flew my mom and me out to Washington D.C. for three days where we met with senators and Dr. C. Everett Koop.

Working with **Children's Miracle Network** has been incredible. I take part in a 24-hour dance marathon every year with other **CMN** kids at USC, and it was through **CMN** I had the honor of meeting with Gov. Pete Wilson who signed the mandatory helmet law during his term in office. Meeting the other **CMN** kids has been inspiring to me because they are all fighters and champions; its great being around them.

Being a part of **CMN** means kids in our community who really need medical help are going to get it at the best hospital there is--Children's Hospital Los Angeles. And it has also given our whole family the opportunity to help other people and become community activists. My parents, sister and brother love helping raise funds for **Children's Miracle Network** because it helps kids who desperately need it.

The people at **CMN** are awesome! They work hard all year putting together telethons, corporate fund raisers, press conferences and community-sponsored events to help kids. The money **CMN** raises also helps provide cutting-edge pediatric research in the area of cancer and other diseases. It really is an honor to be a small part of this great team of people.

So, yes, my life actually has been better because of the accident.

If I could encourage anyone it would be with the plea to not give up hope, no matter how bad things might seem. Just know that with God's help you can accomplish anything; pray often and take things one day at a time. Take comfort in knowing that there are people who really care about you and will do anything to help see you through the rough times.

God bless,

Peter Beal

"So much has been given to me; I have not time to ponder over that which has been denied."

– Helen Keller

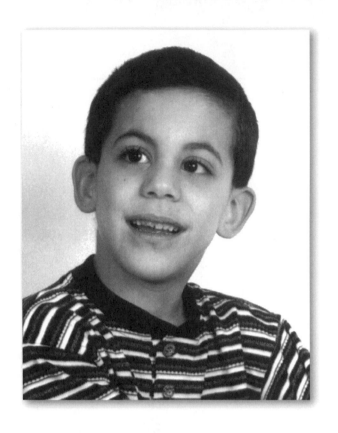

T-BALL PLAYER

...if he had 3 wishes they would be to have a new battery powered jeep, go to Disney World and to the beach.

Daniel Fawcett

Daniel was born on August 13, 1992 at West Virginia University Children's Hospital. He was thirteen weeks premature, weighing only 2 pounds 5 ounces. Shortly after birth, he suffered a severe brain hemorrhage that greatly threatened his survival. Doctors were not optimistic, citing serious potential problems with vision, walking, talking, and other motor skills if he survived.

Daniel has overcome many obstacles in his short life. He has had several surgeries to correct vision and walking problems, and with many hours of physical therapy, he now lives a fairly normal life.

Today, Daniel resides in Grafton, West Virginia with his parents and three sisters. His difficult start in life has made him a very popular child in his community and his biggest asset is obviously his great personality. He will strike up a conversation with anyone and always manages to put a smile on their face.

Daniel Fawcett

Andy Andrews
P.O. Box 2761
Gulf Shores, Alabama   36547

Hi Andy!

Thanks for asking me to be included in your new book called "*Miracles....One At A Time.*" I am only six years old, so my mommy and daddy are helping me write to you.

I have had many problems since I was born and have spent a lot of time in hospitals, visiting doctors, in physical therapy, etc. I am not always able to do what other kids do, but I have done some pretty great things also.

Thanks to Children's Miracle Network, I was invited to visit Washington, D.C. and Disney World as part of the CMN Telethon. While in D.C. , I visited many different places including the White House where I shook hands with President Clinton and Mrs. Clinton. Disney World and the Telethon were great also. I got to see lots of famous people. I also liked flying in airplanes and riding the buses on this trip. It was a super trip!

Your Friend,

Daniel
Daniel Fawcett

P.S. Thank You for helping Children's Miracle Network!

Stephanie, Kaleb and Kinzie

NURSE

...music is her first love. She is also an artist and enjoys doing portrait work and oil paintings. She loves spending the rest of her time with her kids.

Stephanie A. Stebens

Stephanie developed a love for music early in life. She has played the piano since the age of eight and is now accomplished on the guitar, harmonica, and dulcimer. She sings in two church choirs and performs solo music as well.

When Stephanie was 31, she went back to school and became a registered nurse. Then, she continued her education at Marycrest College in Davenport, Iowa for her Bachelor of Science in Nursing degree. Stephanie has put her knowledge and skill to good use. She has been a commission member for the Community Action Agency in Iowa, speaks at events for Children's Miracle Network and Mother's Against Drunk Driving, and recently received an award from the governor for her volunteerism. This is a mother who cares not only for her children, but ours as well.

Stephanie A. Stebens

Andy Andrews
P. O. Box 2761
Gulf Shores, AL 36547

Dear Andy,

I am so honored to be writing you about my miracle. I do feel it is my way of giving hope to others who are experiencing difficult times and it is also my way of healing from the trauma itself.

On June 2, 1998 my life and the lives of my children was irrevocably changed by the decision of a 17 year old girl who decided to get behind the wheel of a truck when she was drunk and angry. My 8-year-old son was out riding his bike when the truck struck him. He was pulled under the truck and dragged over 50 feet down a paved street. I was at home one block away when I received a call from the emergency room. They asked if I had a son named Kaleb. I told them "yes" and they informed me that he had been in an accident and to come to the hospital.

When they allowed me into the exam room I saw a small child with IV's in both arms and legs, the screen from the machine monitoring his heartbeat, oxygen levels and pulse was beeping beside him. When I walked up beside him I could see that his right eye was swollen shut but there was a pillowcase covering the left side of his head. I thought that was strange and wondered why they didn't have sterile gauze or something there instead. Then the Doctor pulled back the covering and it seemed as if time stood still. I felt myself floating above the room and there was a mist filtering in around me.

The voices speaking to me sounded muffled and far away. I wanted to change the channel but I didn't have a remote. What I saw was my baby with a hole in the side of his head. It actually looked as if a bomb had exploded and blown away the side of his face. As a nurse I found myself identifying structures of the brain. Yes, I was sure that was the brain and I knew the pieces of skull should not be sticking out at that particular angle. His left ear was no longer even attached to his face and I could see the lines of muscle tissue going down into his cheek. But then I had to focus my attention on the Doctor who was trying to tell me something I was sure was important. I saw my son look at me and the first thing he said was "I'm sorry, Mommy." I couldn't believe he was alive, let alone able to talk to me. I listened to the Doctor as he explained that this injury was beyond what could be handled locally and he had already called for the life-flight helicopter from Iowa City. They wanted my permission, which I of course gave. All this time I had been trying not to react or let my face show any signs of fear so that Kaleb would not get scared. I knew that if I stayed calm he would too. My heart was hurting so much that I finally had to walk to another side of the room and turn my back so he couldn't see me. It was at this time that our Pastor came up, having just arrived, and put his hand on my shoulder.

I had called him before they took me to see Kaleb. I'm not sure why, but I just thought I might need him. He held me and then went to Kaleb. I knew he was praying over him as I watched him move his hand back and forth over his heart. The helicopter was just landing and everything was moving quickly again. They were getting Kaleb ready to leave and I wanted to kiss him, but there wasn't a spot on him that didn't have a needle in it or was otherwise scraped and bleeding. I finally kissed him on his foot and told him to hang on until I got there.

…Continued

33

Pastor Doug drove me the 60 miles to the hospital in record time. As we drove I experienced all the stages of grief, denial, anger, bargaining. I was sure he would not be alive when we got there. I knew this was my punishment for not being a perfect parent, maybe if I promised to never yell at him again, God would give me another chance. Finally after I was spent and could do nothing more than cry, Pastor Doug told me it was time to pray. There was nothing I could do for Kaleb so I needed to put him in God's hands and trust that God would be there no matter what happened. And I did just that. I closed my eyes and I asked God to take care of my baby and if he would, to please give him back to me because I loved him so much. Even if he wasn't perfect just let him live and give me the strength to handle what needed to be done. At that moment I felt my heartbeat begin to slow, and a warmth began at the top of my head and traveled through my whole body exiting through my fingers and toes. I did not "hear" a voice, but these words were given to me, "Calm down, he is going to be okay. Cool it, he is going to need you later." Even thought I wasn't sure what had happened to me I did calm down and from that point on I did not cry for Kaleb or myself. I felt composed and in control again.

Kaleb underwent 4 hours of surgery to clean 5 rocks and other road debris from inside the brain, close the lining to the brain, plating of the skull fragments together and plastic surgery to cover his skull. When the neurosurgeon came out he had a look of wonder on his face. He told me Kaleb must have a special mission because he was still alive, I knew then that we were in the right hospital and that God was working through these people so Kaleb would survive. The next hurdle we were told was to find enough skin to cover the skull with, as most of it was gone. I went into a bathroom and got down on my knees and I told God I knew that he was going to save Kaleb, but please let them find enough skin so they didn't have to take it from somewhere else. I didn't want him to have to be cut up anywhere else at this point. When the plastic surgeon came out he told us another amazing story. They were cleaning the area of skin to prepare it to be stretched. They had also prepared an area on his chest in case they needed to take muscle to transplant on his face. But when they were cleaning the cheek area they pulled at the tissue and found that most of the missing muscle was rolled inside itself into his cheek. There was enough there to cover the side of his head. They only needed a small skin graft that they took from his scalp. I stayed by Kaleb's side the first 48 hours. On the second day he looked at me with tears in his eyes and asked me if he was going to die. I told him then with certainty that he was not, that God had a special plan for him.

Kaleb came home from the hospital 10 days after the accident but had to have a second surgery to graft skin over his face. During the next 6 weeks we had to go back and forth to the hospital 5 days a week. It was at this time that I began to realize the toll this had all taken on me emotionally. I felt drained, I wasn't sleeping because of the nightmares and sometimes I woke up and just needed to touch Kaleb to be sure he was alive. I explained to a friend, that I felt like I had been on a mission and I needed to be debriefed before going out into the world again. I was also so angry at this young girl who had almost taken my child from me. My oldest child was also feeling neglected by all the attention her brother was getting, but I just couldn't do it any differently. Then came

…Continued

the day my son went back to school. I had a party planned at the end of the day for all the 3rd grade kids with pizza and pop. The news media came to update everyone on Kaleb's recovery also. I didn't see them interview Kaleb so it was a surprise when I watched the stories on the news that night.

I stood in silence when one of the news reporters asked Kaleb how he felt about the young girl who had hit him. I held my breath, afraid of what he might say. I had been feeling particularly bitter, angry and hateful at what her actions had cost me emotionally as well as financially, since I had not worked for almost 5 months. I was afraid that my emotions might have influenced my son, but I was about to learn something very important. I watched as my son paused and thought before he said, "Well, I forgave her, because when I saw her at court she looked sad." I was proud to be Kaleb's mother at that moment. I was also humbled by my son's ability to forgive after the pain and surgeries. How could I place myself above as judge and jury, I had made many mistakes in my life also. I was not ready to forgive her, but I knew I had to try.

At the sentencing hearing I stood before the judge to say my peace to this young girl who is also a mother. I let all of my anger and resentment out in my prepared statement. I admitted that I was having a difficult time forgiving her but that I was finally willing to work on it and with God's help I would succeed. I let Kaleb have the last word since he was the true victim. After telling the judge that his mother wouldn't let him swear, but he would promise to tell the truth he simply said, "I just wanted you to know that I forgave her for running over me."

Since then you would think that things have gone back to normal, but that is not the case. In January I was fired from my job, at the time I was ready to return to work. They apparently couldn't understand why I was traumatized by seeing my son's brain in the ER. But through all the financial worries and medical worries I have decided to trust in God to get us through. And you know what? It has worked! When I need money to pay a bill, a check has appeared in the mail. I don't have a fulltime job, but I am a substitute nurse for the school district and I have worked just enough to make ends meet. I don't have health insurance but there is a new insurance available for working parents that covers children at no cost. Somehow, it has worked out, God has provided.

Before the accident I worked many extra hours to make more money to buy "things". I didn't get to see my children because I worked evenings and they stayed with their grandparents. Now I enjoy being home in the evening and taking them to their activities. I enjoy taking them to school and picking them up. I feel like I have been given a great gift, I witnessed a miracle with my own eyes. I can't say that everyday I am forgiving when I think of that drunk driver, but most days I can. I feel like I have been released from a terrible burden that I carried for years. Everything finally makes sense. I love working with the children at the schools when I do work. For the first time I love going to work and coming home to be with my children. I have found a new relationship with God and I know that I can trust Him to take care of us. I am trying to carry our message of hope to others and also work to make people aware of the real victims in drunk driving accidents. I realized I can't be bitter anymore because there is nothing I can do to put things back the way they were and now I know I wouldn't want to.

…Continued

I feel special that God gave me this child, not once but twice, to love and raise for His special purpose. I pray that our miracle can bring peace to those who may be questioning their faith or trying to make sense out of life. The truth is things just happen, but God is there to help put the pieces of our lives back together and give us the strength to overcome adversity and trying times. I am so fortunate.

I truly believe that God is working through the Children's Miracle network to make miracles happen, one at a time. We have met the most caring loving people at the hospital. They have cried with me and laughed with me. They have taken care of the families emotional needs as well as our physical needs. They, with God's help gave me back my son. I believe by supporting them I can help another family have their miracle also. I have a picture in my room of a baby and the saying is, "Babys are Gods way of saying the world should continue." I want to make sure our babys continue also and that is possible with help from the Children's Miracle Network.

God Bless,

Stephanie A. Stebens

Stephanie A. Stebens

PS. Kaleb decided he didn't want plastic surgery for the scar on his face. He said that the scar looks like a "J" which stands for Jesus and if they changed it no one would know where Jesus healed him. God is good, all the time. All the time, God is good.

"Life is not easy for any of us. Early on in life I decided that I would not be vanquished and that I would remain cheerful in the face of circumstances."

– Rose Kennedy

Rick, Ann, Sarah, Carrie and Chad

...a family who has endured many obstacles. Yet these obstacles make them stronger and closer and tackle the world with their head held high and a smile on their face.

The Mach Family

These three letters from this amazing family will touch your heart. The challenges that might devastate another family, the Machs describe as simply "setbacks". These letters will show the continuously optimistic attitude this family has developed in order to successfully navigate one crisis after another.

Rick is the Manager of the Engineering Department for the city of Sioux City, Iowa. Ann is a seamstress working for a local tailor. Their three children, Sarah, Carrie, and Chad are the wonderful product of their 22-year marriage. During the past year, Rick lost his father and Ann developed breast cancer and yet, their faith and courage remains strong.

"These setbacks," Ann says, "are meant to make us stronger people and better people. We try not to feel sorry for ourselves but to move forward with each new day and make it a better one than the day before."

Rick and Ann Mach

Dear Andy,

I'm sure many people find themselves in the same position we did approximately seven years ago. Our careers were going well. We had three lovely children, and for the most part, we were a very healthy and well-adjusted family. Many would say we were "blessed."

In January of 1993, we experienced our first real roadblock. Our second child, Carrie, who had been experiencing severe stomach cramps for about a month, was diagnosed with cancer. With the doctor's words, "Your daughter has cancer," our life and its purpose took on new meaning.

At first we were overwhelmed with feelings of fear, anger and anxiety. By medical standards, we were told, her chances of survival were not good. We felt hopeless, but soon realized if we let Carrie see our hopelessness, then she definitely would not survive. We needed to maintain a positive attitude through all of this.

A cold chill settled over us as we began the task of preparing ourselves for her surgery and the ensuing chemotherapy and radiation treatments that would follow. We began to read all the books and articles we could find as a means of preparing for this battle, all the while, maintaining a "we can do it" attitude.

We also tried to be as positive as we could to our other two children, Sarah, 11 at the time, and Chad, 7. However, being that we were so focused on Carrie, we have come to realize that they felt a bit neglected. As they mature, we know they now realize those things, those feelings, were a normal progression to whom and what our family was to become.

We have all become stronger by this experience. Through this journey, we have learned how special life really is. We have come to appreciate each day for the joy and disappointments it brings. We have learned to work, live, play and serve others with a passion, for we never know when our time together will end.

Our family, friends, and acquaintances have become more important to us. We have all become more spiritual. We have learned that we get more from giving than from receiving and that the more we give, the more we receive. We have become better Christians who have become closer to God through our experience. The sign of God working spiritually in our lives is shown by an increase in the spirit of cooperation, love and mutual support of fellow Christians. If that is the barometer by which we are judged, then we **are** truly "blessed."

Sincerely,

Rick and Ann Mach

Sarah Mach

Dear Andy,

Nearly seven (7) years ago, my sister, Carrie, was diagnosed with an extremely rare form of cancer. That first year must have been a very difficult time for her. She endured much physical as well as mental and emotional pain. I was no support to her, in fact I hated her. I was so angry that she had this disease. I did not want to touch her, look at her, or even think about her. Obviously, she would receive no comfort from me. I did everything I could to stay away from her. For some insane reason, I believed that it was her fault that she had cancer.

She was frequently in the hospitals for extended periods of time for chemotherapy treatments and my parents would often stay with her. This meant that they were never at home and I became very jealous. These terribly unhealthy feelings continued on for around five (5) years.

Fortunately for Carrie and I, she was able to be treated and receive superior care. The doctors and nurses were so wonderful. They made her comfortable and helped her through many difficult surgeries and chemotherapy and radiation treatments. Thanks to them, a miracle was able to happen.

Through their efforts, Carrie's life has been extended. This has given me the time that I needed to heal and accept what was happening in my life. I learned that being angry was normal and a part of healing. I also learned that cancer was not my sister's or my fault. It was something that happened, although I firmly believe that there is an important reason for it. My sister never gave up on me. She would tell me all the time how much she loved me. No matter how much I would push her away, she would still care about me and try to comfort me. I eventually came to let myself acknowledge that I was living with an extraordinary, beautiful human being.

I learned that cancer can never destroy love or relationships. In fact I have found the exact opposite to be true. My sister is now my best friend. She has taught me more about life than I could have ever thought possible. Life is a wonderful gift and the most fragile concept. Above all she has taught me how to love and truly care about others and myself. I am now more comfortable with who I am and with my relationships with others. I have also been strengthened in my relationship with God. He is at the center of all love .

Everyday is still a continuous battle against the cancer but now we can fight it together. My life will never be the same because I have let myself love and know my brave and courageous sister. Always remember that love conquers all.

Sincerely,

Sarah A. Mach

Carrie Mach

Dear Andy,

I believe few would be able to look at my life and be able to resist cringing. However, looking back, I consider myself to be one of the luckiest people to ever walk the face of this earth. God has blessed me with so much, and every mountain I have climbed has brought me that much closer to His Glory.

When I was nine years old, I learned that I had a tumor in my adrenal gland. The softball sized lump was removed on January 8, 1993 and found to be Adrenal Cortical Carcinoma, an extremely rare cancer. The doctors knew very little about this type of cancer; they decided to bombard it with extremely high doses of chemotherapy. I immediately lost all of my hair and began my own personal six months of hell. After surviving chemo, I began one and a half months of radiation.

One year later, at a check up at the Mayo Clinic in Rochester, Minnesota, I was told I was in remission. I celebrated with family and friends. Unfortunately, our joy was short lived because in May of 1995, I was told that the cancer had come back. I had surgery to remove the lump growing in my lower back, followed by one and a half months of radiation, again. Four months later we learned that this type of cancer has a strong tendency to come back. This time, it was in my skull. It was found in a routine check up at the Mayo Clinic. I again did the routine of surgery and radiation.

Six months went by without a recurrence. Then a year. In March of 1997, though, two tumors were discovered in my liver. I again had to travel to Rochester to have them removed, because no physician in our area would operate on a teenager's liver. Less than a year later, in early February of my freshman year of high school, I felt a lump on my head while in the shower. I passed it off as just a bruise, but as the "bruise" grew, I forced myself to face the truth; my cancer had come back in the front of my head. At the same time, we found a tumor on my thoracic vertebrae. I had both tumors surgically removed with radiation to my spine only. We opted to skip the radiation to my head. That September the growth in the front of my head was back. I once again had it removed, but this time the surgery was followed up by radiation. I luckily went the rest of the school year without a recurrence. However, this past summer, in June of 1999, I had a MRI because my tongue had been swollen. The scan showed a tumor at the base of my skull. It also showed a recurrence on my spine. We had them both radiated, but I was not able to have surgery in either location.

Three months later, in September of my junior year, I began to have trouble with my right leg. I slowly lost feeling in it until it became a chore just to walk. I again denied the truth for about a month. I was afraid there was another tumor on my spine, and that it could paralyze me. I went to our school's Homecoming Dance on Saturday. By Monday, when I finally got in to see the doctor, I needed the assistance of a wheelchair. For my safety and comfort, I was placed in the hospital that day while tests were being run. The tests showed that the tumor was not on my spine, as I had guessed, but pressing on my brain. I underwent surgery on Wednesday. The orange-sized growth was luckily encased and they were able to remove all of it. As I am writing this, I have just begun radiation.

Only today, I was again reminded how my fight continues. We found one more mass in my skull, which I will have removed tomorrow.

Andy, with each battle I have fought, I have only learned to love life more. I don't think of my situation as a burden or a punishment. It is an occasional setback that I can look at as a reminder from God to remember how precious each day is.

From cancer I have learned so much about living. I have seen how beautiful people can be. Through all of this, I have been completely supported by family and friends.

I firmly believe that every soul has a purpose. I believe mine is to remind others to seek enjoyment in every day, to find the beauty in life and each other. Rejoice that you have the chance to fight every battle and experience every obstacle.

I thank you, Andy, for giving me this chance to relay my message. I hope this collection of letters inspires others to keep fighting, and more importantly, to keep smiling. It is a beautiful thing you are doing, and I am honored to be part of it.

Best Wishes,

Carrie Mach

Carrie Mach

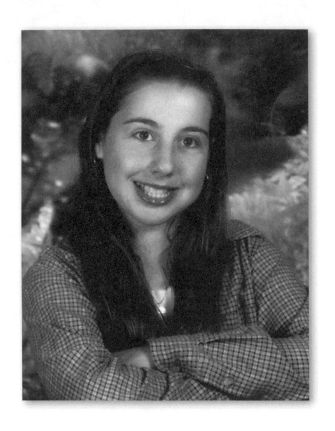

LOVES BEING WITH HER FRIENDS

She loves to listen to music and talk on the phone. If she could turn back time she would go back to the 1950's and see the difference from then and now.

Sara Lynch

One day Sara would like to meet her favorite singer, Mariah Carey. I think Mariah would be the lucky one!

Sara is an outstanding young lady with all the energy and spunk you'd want in a best friend. She loves art and would one day love to create her own comic strip.

Sara loves to dance, and since her surgery and subsequent remission, has been dancing a lot. In fact, regaining her balance and the strength in her legs was a victory that Sara now counts among her proudest achievements.

Sara is a Monopoly shark, as her grandmother often finds out. It is her favorite game and she is good! She also enjoys strawberries and macaroni (but not together) and plans to be a dentist when she grows up.

♥♥♥♥♥♥♥♥♥♥♥♥♥♥♥♥♥ Sara Lynch ♥♥♥♥♥♥♥♥♥♥♥♥♥♥♥♥♥

Andy Andrews
P.O. Box 2761
Gulf Shores, AL 36547

Dear Andy,

My name is Sara Lynch and I'm 13 years old, when I was 11 I found out I had Myasthenia Gravis which is a form of Muscular Dystrophy. This is rare in kids. The doctors at Children's Hospital gave me medicine to help me. But the only hope would be to have surgery to remove my thymas gland. The doctors did not know if this would help or not. This was our only hope of remission.

I've learned that having an illness is very hard to get through. It's hard to get use to the changes when you're sick. I know it was hard for me because of the way I talked I would slur my words, and it was also hard for me to dance. When I did cartwheels and handstands my arm muscles would not support me making it hard for me to do. I use to be able to do all kind of activities. It was difficult because I loved to dance. My leg muscles got very weak. It was hard for me to get in and out of the car, walk, and to get ready for school. There were more changes then these but these were the hardest for me to get through.

When I was going through my surgery it was a hard time for me. My family and especially my friends were there for me they were always there to cheer me up. My 5th grade teacher came into my house to tutor me so that I would not get behind my other 6th graders. My mother came into the class and explained to all my classmates what was going on in my life so that they would not have to ask me a lot of questions.

After my surgery I felt like a new person. I am now able to do the things that for 2 years I could not do. We pray every day that my illness will remain in remission and that I will not have to go on medication again. I am now a cheerleader for the Corona Chargers and I also love to dance. I can participate in all activities now and not have to feel different.

I have found everyone has something wrong with them and that I shouldn't be scared of being different. It could be worse. When I was in the hospital I beat a lot of records. I left the hospital in 42 hours that was one record. Another one was I was one of the youngest people to go in remission 2 months after surgery.

I want to thank all the people at Children's Miracle Network. They have helped me understand that everything would be and continues to be all right. They also helped me realize that I could get through it, and if I had any questions I know I could just ask. I would get the answer right away. Thank you very much for being there. I just want to tell all the people not to give up because you'll make it. If you put yourself down it'll make you feel worse. Keep it up your day will come too. I love to help other people and if I can make a difference in someone else's life that would make me feel real good.

Sara Lynch
Sara Lynch

Joe and Marta

BUSINESSMAN

...co-founded CHILDREN'S MIRACLE NETWORK and produced the annual telethon. Under his leadership, CMN has helped raise over a billion dollars for children's hospitals in the United States and Canada.

Joseph G. Lake

I am very proud to count this man as one of my friends. I met Joe for the first time backstage at a Children's Miracle Network event and was instantly mesmerized by the passion he generated for the work he was doing. He introduced me to children, athletes, entertainers, and any number of other volunteers who were committed, like Joe and his wife Marta, to making life better for others.

Joe was named Young Businessman of the Year in 1972 by the National Junior Chamber of Commerce. Ten years later, with his partner, Mick Shannon and entertainers Marie Osmond and John Schneider, he co-founded the international Children's Miracle Network to raise funds for 170 not-for-profit children's hospitals and to create awareness of children's physical and emotional health and welfare issues. Under his leadership and with his partner, Mick Shannon, CMN has now raised approximately 1.4 billion dollars for children's hospitals in the United States and Canada.

Joseph G. Lake

Mr. Andy Andrews
P.O. Box 3709
Gulf Shores, AL 36547

Dear Andy:

What an honor to be asked to write a letter for this new, wonderful book! Your friendship and association over the past 17 years mean a great deal to me.

As I have retired from the day- to- day activity of The Children's Miracle Network, I find that I have more time to do the things that I want to do. I am spending more time with my family. As you know, I have been married to Marta for 35 years and we have 6 children.

I have met many very special "miracle kids" over the years, and in trying to find just one to feature, I thought I would tell you a story that few people know.

When Marie Osmond, John Schneider, Mick Shannon and I started The Children's Miracle Network in 1983, we were trying to decide which children's charities we would want our efforts to support.

Our #4 child, Marcine, was born November 6th, 1975. When Marci was only 3 years old, she got very sick. We had her into the doctor several times over a few day period and we were told that she had a tough strain of flu and that with rest and lots of liquids she would be fine in a few days.

One day, her fever was real high and we took her back to the doctor and once again was told that we needed to keep giving her aspirin, cold baths and lots of liquid to drink.

That night, for some reason, I could not sleep. (I never have trouble sleeping) I woke up in the middle of the night and checked on Marci. I went into her room. She was burning up with fever and she was sweating bad and I could not get her to respond to me.

Marta got up and we rushed Marci to Primary Children's Medical Center here in Salt Lake City. (Today, Primary Children's is the CMN hospital in Utah).

We were seen very fast in the emergency room and when the doctor looked at her he said that he was convinced that she had a major bladder infection that was affecting her kidneys and that was causing the infection and high fever.

They rushed her into surgery to repair the damage and clean out the infection. The operation went well and in a few days she was back being the fun, bright and "well" little 3 year old girl.

7972 South Willow Circle
Sandy, Utah 84093

Phone: (801) 943-7830   Fax: (801) 942-6158

The doctor told us that had we not gotten Marci to the hospital that night, she would have died in her sleep. She was on the verge of a coma when I went in to check on her.

Talk about "Miracles". There were two of them that night....first, it was
a miracle that I woke up, and second, Primary Children's Medical Center was my "Miracle" hospital.

In 1983 when Marie, John, Mick and I decided on a children's charity, I really wanted it to be Children's Hospitals. Today, there are 170 Children's hospitals affiliated with CMN and we have raised over $1.4 billion for these very special hospitals throughout North America in our first 17 years.

As I have met the "Miracle Kids" and their families over the years I have felt what they have been through and marvel at the way these kids can overcome so many different medical problems. My heart goes out to these families, you see........... I have a 22 year old Miracle child of my own.

Kindest Personal Regards,

Joseph G. Lake
Co-Founder
Children's Miracle Network, Retired

"Our deepest fear is not that we are inadequate. Our deepest fear is that we are powerful beyond measure. It is our light not our darkness, that most frightens us. We ask ourselves, who am I to be brilliant, talented, and fabulous? Actually, who are you not to be? You are a child of God. Your playing small doesn't serve the world. There is nothing enlightened about shrinking so that other people won't feel insecure around you. We are born to make manifest the Glory of God that is within us. It's not just in some of us, it's in everyone, and as we let our own light shine, we consciously give other people permission to do the same. As we are liberated from our own fear, our presence automatically liberates others."

– Nelson Mandela

Kristina and Dominique

ELEMENTARY TEACHER

...a high spirited person. She has lived through a rough time in her life, but has survived and come out stronger and wiser.

Kristina Crump Minst

Kristina and I talked one afternoon by phone. I asked her, "What has been the hardest part of this ordeal for you?"

"Not knowing what was going to happen," she answered simply. "But," she continued, "I suppose that has also been a blessing."

She recently married La Mar Minst, a man she met in April of 1996, right before Dominique went through her roughest period. They have been together through all of it and now have five children between them.

Kristina's parents, Jim and Olivia Young, also live close by. They have been a huge part of the support system throughout this experience as have other friends and church members. Kristina teaches sixth grade in Ventura where she has enough love and energy for other children as well!

Kristina Crump Minst

Andy Andrews
P. O. Box 2761
Gulf Shores, AL 36547

Dear Andy,

Dominique was born on May 28, 1994. She was a beautiful baby. I was a single mother at the time, having recently been separated from my husband. D'Andre, my two year old, toddled along behind me as I took care of our new arrival.

As a sixth grade teacher, my life was hectic, but manageable. In fact, things were going along quite well until one evening while holding the children. I noticed several small lumps on Dominique's skull. She was three months old.

Early the next morning, I bundled her up and made the trek to our pediatrician who directed us immediately to a local dermatologist for a biopsy. Without delay, the results came back. Dominique was diagnosed with a rare form of lymphoma. At least, this type cancer is extremely uncommon in a baby. To this day, Dominique is the youngest patient in the world to ever be diagnosed with this particular problem.

Interestingly, I did not panic. I went quickly into an action mode. What do we need to do? Where do we need to go? We lost the feelings of depression in a flurry of activity. I was looking for answers!

After extensive testing at Children's Hospital of Los Angeles, it was determined that, in addition to the tumors on her skull, Dominique also had tumors on her kidneys and a tumor the size of an egg on her uterus. Biopsy on the internal growths required surgery, but nothing so extensive as the operation that readied my child for chemotherapy.

Because her veins were so small and unable to hold the needle necessary to administer the cancer fighting drugs, doctors placed a tube through Dominique's chest directly into her heart muscle...and the technique worked. We watched as the tumors shrunk and disappeared.

For eighteen months, my baby seemed normal and healthy. Life had returned to its old pace when suddenly, we were shaken again. The cancer came back.

This time we faced an even more serious situation and were told that a bone marrow transplant was the only option. Having heard stories of families who searched endlessly for a donor match, I had nightmares of sifting through hundreds of thousands of possibilities to save my daughter. And then, a miracle.

D'Andre, now four, was the first test possibility...and he matched. A real trooper, he marched into the hospital to save his sister. He never cried and the transplant was a success.

...Continued

During this time, Dominique endured a three-month stay in the hospital. My dad split shifts with me staying with Dominique. We had to scrub down like a surgeon and put on a spacesuit to be in the same room with her. It was hard to never touch her skin, never kiss her face. We had to be upbeat. She was not old enough to know what was wrong, only that something was!

We slept at Ronald McDonald House to be near Dominique, but I also had to continue to work. Daddy and I were both exhausted, but the doctors, nurses, and staff at Children's were phenomenal. Supportive and compassionate, they made our ordeal as easy as possible.

The transplant was quite obviously successful. Dominique is in kindergarten now, a happy, healthy little girl. So what did we learn? We learned to be grateful for every day. We are thankful for the kindness shown our family during and beyond a scary time in our lives. Many people pulled together and worked to save a little girl who will now grow up to be…what? An artist, a mother, an astronaut, a friend, a doctor or nurse, a world changer! She is special already for she has been given the gift of a fighting spirit. This tough time in our lives has let us all see the "stuff" of which we are made. And we are glad.

Sincerely,

Kristina Crump

"No act of kindness, no matter how small, is ever wasted."

– Aesop, "The Lion and the Mouse"

FUTURE COMPUTER PROGRAMMER

...would like to be in Star Wars and be an X-wing pilot. He plays this game on his computer because he has the choice to be a good or bad character.

Ryan Donnelly

Look at the picture. One can tell that this is a fun kid to be around! Ryan's favorite foods are chicken, bananas, and sausage pizza. He would like to be a video game tester when he grows up in order to play all the new games before they are released. He likes Pokemon, clown fish, and would like to find out how ants lift heavy things.

Ryan lives in New Hampshire with his dad who is the best carpenter in the world and his mom, a terrific physical therapist. He has two sisters, Erin and Leisha. I asked Ryan what his sisters were like. He said, "They like beanie babies, and they like to fight with each other!" I really like this kid!

Ryan Donnelly

Dear Andy,

I'm very glad to do this letter for your book. I think that its a wonderful experience, and a great thing to do.

In my life there have been many chalenges, great, and small. One of the greatest chalenges was raising me as a baby.

With "Brittle Bones" I was very fragile, I was constantly breaking for fracturing bones. I also had severe curves in the bones in my legs, so I was unable to sit up. Foortunatly, a few years later, metal rods were put in my legs, my tonsals and adnoids were taken out, and tubes were put in my ears. All of these surgerys and more, really helped me out.

Another part of my life has been C.M.N. With their annual fundrasers and telethons, they have helped doctors, who help kids like me.

Lastly, my advice to other people with my, or any other condition is to keep going no matter what.

Sincerelly,
Ryan Donnelly

...enjoys talking, dancing and swimming. She would love to learn to swing dance and would like to be a writer or journalist to write all about her experience and help others.

Daniella Fortuna

Dani told me she was an "enfant unique". She assures me that this means "only child" in French. Unique, in its English translation, is a good word to describe Dani as well. Born with a birthmark that would hinder the personality of most kids, she has flourished. Her family and friends have been constant encouragers.

Dani is a dancer and choreographer dedicated to creating new moves and expressions and she has used her desire to help other children to become a gifted public speaker. It is on the stage, however, where Dani really shines. Acting is more than just a hobby for her. It is a passion that is currently directing the steps of her future. For Dani, acting is not only a way of expressing herself, it is a way to encourage others to look beyond the surface and see what is inside.

~ DANI ~

Mr. Andy Andrews
P.O Box 2761
Gulf Shores, AL, 36547

Dear Andy,

First before anything, I would like to thank you for asking me to be a part of your book. I'm very honored that you are interested in my story, and I take pleasure in sharing it with you. Though my experience of having a birthmark was difficult it has helped me to grow stronger as a person, and brought my family closer. I've learned to have faith always, and to keep a positive attitude, and I truly do believe in those little things called Miracles. I was raised to always be confident, and try my best, and most importantly not to judge people by the outer appearance. "It's the inside that counts!" When I was little I probably didn't realize what was wrong......I was a pretty HAPPY and SMILEY little girl, but of course there was the occasional stares, or comments, and due to my birthmark my vision is blurred in my left eye.

 The miracle of all this is what it became, and what opportunities I have been blessed with. When I was 8 (At that time I had already been through about 3 surgeries) I was invited to take part in the Childrens Hospital Los Angeles/ Childrens Miracle Network annual broadcast. I participated in the broadcast with other patients, and their families, and many celebrities. I have had the chance to meet with many different people, most importantly the patients. It wouldn't be possible to meet all of these wonderful people if it weren't for Childrens Miracle Network. So for not only giving me the chance to meet people, and share my story in hopes of helping others, but for helping all of the 4 million children every year, I would like to say THANK YOU. And I LUV YOU!

Currently I am a child ambassador for Childrens Hospital Los Angeles, and continue to help raise funds on behalf of Childrens Hospital, the hospital that I owe so much to. I feel that by sharing my story, I am giving back to the Hospital for all they have done for me, and what they continue to do for children everywhere. The patients are very courageous and inspiring, the staff very special, and the doctor's are brilliant, my doctor, Dr. John Reinisch is my hero, and my friend. My life is very good right now, I've just started high school, made lots of new friends, study acting, and enjoy spending time with my friends, and my family, and my work at the hospital will always be a priority, honor, and special part of my life.

I believe that when you are faced with a challenge, you must always remember to keep your faith, hope, courage, and trust that things will work out for you. Marie Osmond and I were talking and she said, "You know, God makes everything happen for a reason", And I believe I was meant to help, and encourage others.

Andy, thank you again for allowing me to be part of your book. I wrote a special poem, "Miracles", because I hope that maybe it will help someone who's struggling, or going through a hard time. Thank you again.

Sincerely,

Dani

Daniella (Dani) Fortuna

Miracles

Staying Strong and Praying keeps love in our hearts;
And when one of these happens, a new life forms and starts;
A miracle is when:
A beautiful child is born
A miracle is when:
A second chance is formed
A miracle is when:
Something bad becomes something good;
When the little child who never walked
Tried and found he could
Miracles in a sense do happen by themselves;
But all the strength and nourishment can always be of help;
So when you're thinking about giving up;
Remember to hold on;
You never know when the saddest hymn
Could turn into a happy song.
So don't ever stop believing
And bad times won't seem so long.

Daniella Fortuna

Horacio, Roland, Aurora, Roli and Kadante

MARTIAL ARTS EMPOWERING FAMILY

...dedicated to empowering humanity one student at a time. They believe that only through proactive involvement in the everyday lives of others can we create a better world for our children.

Aurora Ferrer

The following letter is one of my favorites. In these words one can find wisdom, courage, attitude, and character. It has been written: To whom much is given, much is expected. The ordinary person would not consider the Ferrer family recipients of "much". But they have used their situation to learn, grow, and teach others.

Roland, Roli's father, and Aurora own and operate Kadan Martial Arts and Development Center in Garden Grove, California. They are active in the Olympic sport of Taekwondo and have put seven people on the United States national team.

Roland, a 7th Degree Black Belt, has been featured on ESPN, while Aurora, a 2nd Degree Black Belt, is the founder of Kadan's Women's Empowerment Program. They are active in their community and were awarded the Police Athletic League Volunteers of the Year Award in 1997.

Aurora Ferrer

Kadan Martial Arts & Development Ceneter

11887 Valley View St. • Garden Grove • Ca. • 92845
Tel. (714) 890-0080 • Fax (714) 890-0085 • http://lugani.com/kadan

Andy Andrews
P.O. Box 2761
Gulf Shores, Al. 36547

Andy,

We have been graced with two beautiful children Kadante and Roli. They have each brought us many important gifts.

Roli was born with a birth anomaly called Total Colon Hircshprung's Disease. At the age of 3 1/2 weeks he had an iliostomy preformed. The iliostomy brought his small intestine through his abdomen so that he could stool into a bag. I remember walking into his NICU room and wondering how I would see my precious baby. I saw light and love. I saw his iliostomy as that which saved his life and therefor it was beautiful. He was beyond perfect, he was a fighter.

The hospital psychologist came to council my husband and myself during Roli's first hospitalization. She said that it was normal to ask "Why me?" And to be angry with God for this injustice. She said that in time we would get past those feelings. Ironically those feelings had never entered our hearts. We believed then and continue to believe now that Roli's challenge was a gift not a punishment. We believed that we were being given an enormous life lesson in the form of this little angel.

Roli was in and out of the hospital frequently. (10 times in 2 years) Our first Christmas was at Children's Hospital Los Angeles a CMN hospital in California. It was a very scary time for us but again Roli gave us the gift of love. Being together was what Christmas was all about it did not matter where.

When Roli was to undergo his final surgery we had to decide whether or not to insert a G-tube into his stomach to bypass oral feedings. This was a precautionary measure to help minimize dehydration and malnutrition post surgery. My husband and I didn't sleep for over a month. We agonized over the "best" choice. We wanted so badly to do what was best for our baby. I remember feeling that we may not need to subject him to this final surgery, that I loved him with a bag and I was sure he would find a special lady to love him as a man. Then one night I dreamt I was sitting in my kitchen and Roli was across the table from me. He was a handsome and strong young man. He asked me, "mother why didn't you give me the chance to live without this bag?" I realized then that my fears were real but they were selfish. I had to focus on what Roli would want as a man, not what I felt safe giving to him as a mother.

Roli has not been hospitalized in over a year. He is active, strong, and happy. He has given us the tools we needed to create excellence in our lives. He constantly reminds of the importance to be thankful for all that we have and the strength to understand that No is just Maybe in disguise.

My wish for families undergoing serious illness is that they hold the strength and beauty of their love even through the uncertainty and fear. That they find hope in that which may seem hopeless, That they believe in miracles for they are all around us, that they question everything and be proactive as care givers, That they find the beauty in the most unexpected place, that they allow the beauty and strength reflected in their child's eyes find a home within their hearts.

Sincerely,

Aurora Ferrer

...he is a very busy and wonderful person. He is the "Ambassador" for the hospital and for programs that are aimed at schools, clubs and academic institutions.

Robert K. Wilson, Jr., MD

Dr. Bob, as he is affectionately known to his patients, graduated from the University of Alabama in 1959. He attended medical school at the Medical College of Alabama, now University of Alabama in Birmingham. Among the positions Dr. Bob has held include Chief of Pediatrics at Maxwell Air Force Base in Montgomery, Alabama and President of the Florida Public Health Association in 1987.

Dr. Bob is currently the Director of the Department of Pediatrics at Sacred Heart Children's Hospital in Pensacola, Florida. He and his wife have been married for forty-two years and have four sons and two grandchildren. They have lived in Pensacola since 1968 where Dr. Bob, a self professed "people person", enjoys hunting and fishing with his family and friends.

UNIVERSITY OF
FLORIDA

College of Medicine
Department of Pediatrics - Sacred Heart

Sacred Heart Children's Hospital
5151 N. Ninth Avenue
Pensacola, FL. 32504
Phone: (850) 416-7658
Fax: (850) 416-6708

Andy Andrews
Post Office Box 2761
Gulf Shores, AL 36547

Dear Andy,

"Dr. Bob would you please write a note about a 'miracle kid' (Champion) that you recall that meant the most to you?" Tall order, Andy, as my involvement goes back 12 or 13 years with intensification when I was appointed Director of the Pediatric Residency Program at Sacred Heart Children's Hospital in December 1988 and was elected to the Board of Directors of the Sacred Heart Foundation which coordinates and sponsors Children's Miracle Network.

When I think of 2-4 children per year for 11 years, you can appreciate my reticence to pick only one.

There's a young man that I'll always remember every time CMN airs who succumbed to his lifelong disease — cystic fibrosis at age 25 a couple of years ago. He had been a patient at Sacred Heart as a baby and had multiple admissions over the years which is not unusual when one has such a malady.

When a young child he'd been a "miracle kid" and then when he was 13 or so he was a co-host. The local televison and hospital celebrities so much enjoyed the experience they shared with this special boy. He was at his post encouraging foiks "to make miracles happen" and he literally was up the entire 21 hours!

After he died the following CMN featured and honored him and over several minutes showed clips from his past and for me to have had an opportunity to watch it and to relive that event when Eddie was a co-host was a profound experience indeed.

I know I didn't see him every time he was in the hospital, especially after he was no longer a child and adult pulmonologists became his doctors, but when I'd see his mom or dad they'd tell me his whereabout and I'd visit him, incredibly to derive encouragement and inspiration and to become a stronger and better person. I never left his bed side without receiving a benefit. Later I'd reflect on the visit and typically my eyes would moisten because of sadness and because of joy.

Because of his condition he was never an athlete, never a laborer, never a "winner" in the eyes of the world. But Eddie Murphy was a Champion and he was my friend and I'll always miss him

Sincerely,

"Dr. Bob" Wilson

Robert K. Wilson, Jr., M.D.
Director, Pediatric Residency Program

RKWjr:sbs

"You can't wring your hands and roll up your sleeves at the same time."

– Michelle Brown

...enjoys studying the bible and applying it to her everyday life. She loves to draw, play hide and seek, and cook omelettes and pasta.

Cheryl Humble

It is a characteristic of people like Cheryl to focus on the future, not the past; the good, not the bad. When I read Cheryl's letter, I was not surprised to notice that she had virtually neglected to mention her physical problems. Noting the reference to her right hand, I called her father, Jack, at home and asked, "What, exactly, happened to Cheryl's hand?"

"Her hand?" he said. "That was the least of it."

When Cheryl was born, her legs were literally tied into knots. Her right arm, hand, and fingers were twisted and turned. Through the years, she endured and prospered through more than twenty operations. Her father is clearly proud of Cheryl. Her faith and cheerful disposition continue to be the hallmark of her personality.

cheryl humble

Dear Andy,

I think that the hardest trial Ive ever had was realizing that facing life on my own is worthless, but facing Life with Jesus is Pure Joy. I guess it may sound strange to some people but looking back at my life, all my hardest times have been when ive tried to get through life on my own strength.

As a little girl I can remember being truly happy, even at the Hospital I was happy, I loved the nurses, I met great people where no one was judged on looks, no one was made fun of because there was no standard of a perfect person. I know some of my best times have been in the Hospital.

At home I was Home Schooled by my mom along with my 2 brothers and 4 sisters, one of them being my twin sister Crystal, so I wasn't really exposed to any negative behavior as a kid.

When I was 13 me and Crystal started at a public school in eigth grade, our 1st time ever being away from Home School. I can remember everyone being so nice to us, I cant remember once being made fun of but I can remember looking at myself and being ashamed. I had surgery on my right hand that year and after the cast came off I would hide my hand from people so no one would see the scars and deformities. This was the 1st time I ever felt I needed to hide my problems, so it began to develop all kinds of insecurities for me.

By the time I hit my sophomore year in High School I was well on the road to hating myself. I was trying to present myself as being "normal" without realizing that no one had ever rejected me for just being "me." At this time I started pushing people away from me, I was scared to let people get too close. I started getting depressed a lot, and I can remember sitting on my bed wondering what it felt like to be happy, I knew happiness was out there and I longed for it.

One night I went out with friends and got completely drunk, and for the first time in a long time I felt happy so I thought "Here it is, I've found Happiness." But after a year or more of temporary happiness I knew there had to be something more to life. If anything my life was worse, I was moody, constantly depressed, my family thought I hated them, And I hated who I had become and I longed for that childlike happiness I had in the hospital.

That summer I went to a weeklong camp with Crystal, It was a Bible Camp and everything I heard there I wanted, everything that people had I desired. One night the preacher stood there preaching and I felt like he was talking directly to me, I knew I had to let Jesus back in my life, I fought it so hard that I was finally brought to my knees. That summer changed my life, I was not perfect, I was not all of a sudden a wonderful person. I didn't get that mushy "I've found Jesus" feeling, but I had something to live for and that made a huge difference in my life.

One day I was sitting in class and I got called to the office. My mom was there and she told me that the Childrens miracle Network had called and If I wanted to, I could go to Disney World and washington to meet the President. I had never even flown before so It turned out to be an awesome trip. I had so much fun, I met mickey mouse for the 1st time, and I got to fly in an airplane (I got my plastic pilot wings), and Disney was something Id always wanted to do, And meeting the President and his wife made some great memories. The best part of the trip was being in a group of people again who werent looking to be perfect, they were just perfectly thrilled to be alive. On that trip I found that childlike happiness id Been looking for and made friends that will touch my life forever.

Thanks again Andy for what your doing with this Book.
God Bless

Cheryl
Humble

MAJOR BASEBALL FAN

...would like to play baseball and be on the Boston Red Sox team as a pitcher. He is a big fan and claims they are the best in the league. He has a pretty good throw but says it could still be improved.

Cory Garwacki

I talked to Cory and his mom over the phone one day for over an hour. They are happy, positive people, so naturally, I had a blast. Cory lives in a small town in Massachusetts with his mom, dad, and sister, Sarah. He has a dog named Otis and a rabbit, Clover.

Cory's favorite holiday by far is Christmas. The main reason he loves Christmas he explained, is the feeling of "family togetherness". He said, "With all the goodies and food available, it's a perfect holiday for me because I'm the one who likes to eat!"

I am looking forward to watching Cory fulfill his enormous potential as he grows up. He wants to be an Emergency Medical Technician and a famous author. My bets are all on Cory. This is one great kid!

CORY GARWACKI

Andy Andrews
P. O. Box 2761
Gulf Shores, AL 36547

Dear Mr. Andrews,

Thanks for the opportunity to tell my story. I am obviously relying on the memory of my Mom and Dad because my own memory of the day I was born is hazy! It was January 19, 1987 and several hours after I arrived, I vomited amniotic fluid (the stuff that keeps you safe while you are inside your Mom). Within hours, the doctors had discovered that almost all my intestine was missing. My parents were told that I would probably not survive.

Mom and Dad were given two options. The first was to do nothing in which case I would have died within two weeks. The second choice was to insert a central intravenous line for nutrition and a tube into my stomach for medication. This procedure, my parents were told, would eventually damage my liver and kidneys beyond repair. I would probably die by the age of two. There had never been a successful transplant of the intestines. My parents immediately decided to have me connected to the lifelines anyway.

I spent almost my entire first year of life in the hospital. At age one, I began vomiting severely and was admitted to Presbyterian Hospital in New York for a bowel tapering procedure. I had been born with 2.1 inches of intestine, but when the doctors operated, they assumed the numbers had been recorded incorrectly. I had, they determined, 21 inches of intestine. But the numbers had not been in error. My intestine, for some reason, had grown.

By three, I still could not eat very much by mouth. I was hospitalized more often than not and the central line, which was keeping me alive, also kept me open to constant infections. At the Pittsburgh Children's Hospital there exists one of the only Short Gut Clinics in the world. It was there that they decided to perform a specialized tapering surgery on me that had only been done twice before. It had not been successful in either instance, and in one case, the child died.

Well, the operation was a success and within a few months, though still on IV support, I was eating normal food. Interestingly, during surgery, I was found to have 50 inches of intestine. Now understand: the intestine does not normally grow. I had been getting nightly injections of growth hormones for a long time and the doctors thought this was partially responsible.

...Continued

When I was eleven, I wasn't growing or gaining weight like I should. I was getting sick a lot and the doctors, my parents and I decided that this operation needed to be done again. This particular operation had never been repeated on anyone before. During this 14 hour operation, the doctors found I now had 100 inches of intestine and soon I was taken off all IV feedings. I now receive all my nutrition by eating normally. My sister, Sarah, says I don't eat normally though because I eat all the time! Since my intestine doesn't absorb nutrition in a normal way, I do have to eat constantly—at least every hour.

I am in the seventh grade now. I still have a tube in my stomach that I get twenty-five doses of medication daily, but that's cool because it was recently reduced from seventy! I love the Boston Red Sox, fishing, cars, reading, and writing stories. I want to learn CPR and become an Emergency Medical Technician when I grow up. So many people have helped me, I'd like to learn how to help someone else.

I have been constantly in and out of the hospital my whole life. I have missed a lot of school and a lot of time with my friends. This experience, though tough at times, is all I know. Don't feel sorry for my family or me. (Did I tell you I got to meet the President of the United States?) We are a happy bunch. We go through a lot together and we are always there for each other. Even my teenage sister sits with me through hours of tests and procedures so I won't have to go through it alone. I consider myself a very lucky kid. I have great friends and a family who loves me very much. And I love them too! We are also grateful for the doctors and nurses at the Bay State Medical Children's Hospital. They have been terrific. Because of their care and concern, my family has been motivated to help them in any way we can.

Any money given to CMN in this area benefits my friends at this hospital so we work hard. We do walk-a-thons, dances, and raffles. I also appear on the CMN telethon every year. I have a great, fun, and happy life.

Your friend,

Cory Garwacki

Cory Garwacki

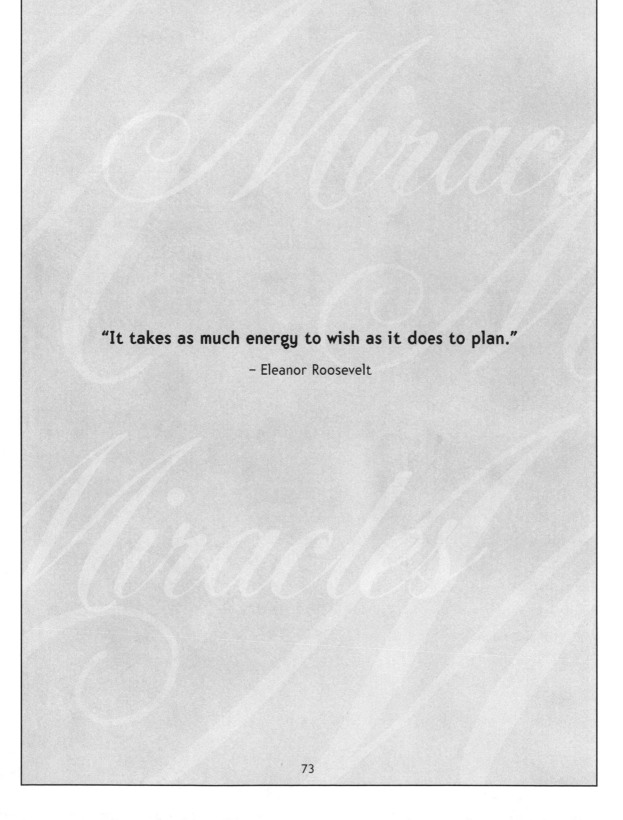

"It takes as much energy to wish as it does to plan."

– Eleanor Roosevelt

CREATED HER OWN BOARD GAME "LIFEPOLY"

...her game is a combination of Monopoly and Life. It is based on the actual streets where she lives.

Annie O'Donnell

Annie was born with multiple congenital conditions involving the heart, gastrointestinal tract, trachea, spine, and kidneys. Within the first three hours of her life, she was transported to Children's Hospital for an emergency tracheotomy to create an opening to her windpipe, which allowed her to breath.

She is fourteen now and a beautiful young lady. She loves to play basketball and golf, talk on the phone with her friends, and play with her kittens. Annie is proud to have helped start the Children's Hospital Teen Volunteer Program that now has well over one hundred participants. Annie O'Donnell is an inspiration to us all, but especially to the hospitalized youngsters who may be facing what Annie has already overcome.

Annie O'Donnell

Mr. Andy Andrews
P.O. Box 2761
Gulf Shores, AL ~ 36547

Dear Andy,

Thank you so much for letting me share my story. I am very honored to write in this publication of *Miracles... One @ A Time*. I , feel that anyone can learn or benefit from my personal experiences and life.

Ever since I can remember, I was called the "Miracle Baby." This is becoming more apparent to me, as I continue to grow. I will let you in on some background. Roughly two hours after I came into this world, I had my first operation. To date, I have had over thirty surgeries. Two of those operations have been open heart and spinal fusion.

Although I do not remember all of them because I was so young, I have became a better person ; over the past years, I have worried less, which is good! I have high gratefulness for my doctors and all the nurses who cared for me. My family also played a key role and I hold them in my highest esteem and love.

The greatest obstacle I overcame was my inability to talk and to comprehend my family and friends. Due to my illness, I had a tracheostomy until I was five. Before, I would communicate with my family and friends by sign language. On June 31, 1986, my trachea finally came out. I COULD TALK! Well.. Not exactly.. I had many specialist and my parents help me with my speech. I started school when I was six. I then had a speech pathologist at my school who worked with me everyday. from first through sixth grade She not only helped me to speak, write, but learn a lot about others. Through my school years, I was in special education until I was in seventh grade. Without these people teaching me, I would **Never Never Never** be where I am, or who I am today. Now, I am a junior in a private catholic high school, I have been soaring, and am on the honor role.

My life has changed ever since my illness. I would get depressed sometimes because I was not like everyone else. As I have grown up , I realize that I really am lucky that this has happened to me. It has changed me into a more compassionate caring person. I have learned not to judge people by their looks, or by their illness, because if people do that, they are missing out on a lot. They are not giving such people a to be chance to known by their inner being.

Ever since I was little, I never would give up. Through everything, I would keep going, because, if I were to stop, I would fall. When times were tough, I would sometimes go get my stuffed bear and hug it, listen to music, talk with friends or just dream about life after this obstacle or situation.

What I would like to say to the Children's Miracle Network??? Without their help, research, money, doctors, nurses, technology, I would probably wouldn't be here today. In 1996, I was honored to take part in the Children's Miracle Network "Champions Across America." Those children who were chosen went to Washington D.C., to meet President Clinton and tour Washington, D.C. . I was one of four kids, who got to place the wreath on the Tomb of the Unknown Solder. Then, we flew down to Florida for the live Telethon. Through this trip, I met all kinds of beautiful kids who have experienced some sort of illness but have overcome their challenges. I learned so much about them, and each has a unique place in my heart. I would like to give thanks to CMN for the "Trip of a Life time" for their support throughout my life, and to every sick child in this country. **You truly do make a difference**!

In my seventeen years , every surgery or sickness I have had, has been performed at the Local Children's Hospital in Omaha. Their staff has not only been compassionate, caring, loving, but they are also now a part of my life and family. Again, without each and every person, I would not be here today. I have been volunteering at Children's for four years now, and I can not express how happy I am, to be helping other children. I am trying to give back to Children's Hospital little by little.

My Motto is ~
"Never give up, believe in God and have Faith, and Everything will work out."

Annie O'Donnell

"I was always looking outside myself for strength and confidence, but it comes from within. It is there all the time."

– Anna Freud

A FAMILY THAT LOVES THE OUTDOORS

...their lives are filled with wonderful children and great companionship. They love the great outdoors and enjoy doing these things as a family and as much as possible.

Brandon, Rita, Andrew and Alan

Alan and Rita Shapiro

This letter was one of the most moving I have ever read. These words, I believe, will take you into the heart of a parent.

Alan has lived in Los Angeles all his life. Rita, on the other hand, was born in Ecuador and moved to the United States around age two or three. Her family subsequently settled in Los Angeles where she became a United States citizen at age sixteen. Alan and Rita were married on January 16, 1993 after seven years of dating. Alan was Rita's boss at the time, though they now work at two different, very busy, Los Angeles law firms.

The Shapiro's life revolves around their family. Brandon is now in kindergarten and has mastered the computer. Andrew is in pre-school, and though he is rather shy, can carry on a conversation with any adult! Camping, boating, snow skiing, and bike riding are high on their list of activities. This family, quite literally, does everything together. Recently, Brandon joined a T-Ball team. Wouldn't you know it—Alan helps coach, Rita is the team Mom, and Andrew is the team's biggest supporter.

Alan and Rita Shapiro

Andy Andrews
P.O. Box 2761
Gulf Shores, AL 36547

Hi Andy,

We have two great boys, Brandon and Andrew. They are the best things that could ever have happened to us.

Unfortunately, our boys were born with congenital heart defects. Brandon (6), our oldest, was born with Aortic Valvular Stenosis. And, Andrew (3), our baby, was born with Tetrology of Fallot. Brandon was just barely 24 hours old when we were hit with the devastating news. Andrew was a couple of days old before a murmur was detected. Having experienced the "devastating blow" 21/2 years earlier with Brandon did not make it easier to handle the news the second time around.

Both of our sons have already had heart procedures. Brandon had an Aortic Volvuloplasty at six months old. He is going to need open-heart surgery in a few years and possibly another open-heart surgery as he approaches adulthood. Andrew had open-heart surgery at six months old and he too will likely need another one in a few years with the possibility of more than one.

At ages six and three, our boys are presently doing well. They are growing normally, they are very active, very artistic and they are very popular with their teachers and fellow students. They both are extremely loving and they are as smart as whips.

Our boys are very special. God gave us special children and we have therefore become a special family with special challenges and concerns. Nobody knows or understands what this involves unless they experience the circumstances we have experienced with our boys.

Few people will ever really know the shear terror, the agony, the absolute panic, the horrible sickening feeling brought on by the moments approaching the separation from our baby, our little helpless baby, as the nurse takes our baby away from us. The nurse does it lovingly and tenderly and with all the care that she can. But it is our baby she is removing from our arms. It is our baby going in for what they have told us is "high risk" surgery. And we realize we are utterly and completely helpless.

It starts off with the requirement that we sign the "informed consent" form. The doctors will not operate unless we sign the form. If we do not sign the form, they will not do the only thing that can be done to extend the life of our baby. Our baby will die if we do not sign the informed consent form. As we read the form, it clearly states that our baby has a 97% chance of surviving the surgery. Our brains tell us that there is a three per cent chance that our child will die while on the operating table. Suddenly that 3% is not good enough. The chances of death during surgery are too high. We don't want there to be a three percent chance of death. That three percent looms much too large. We want there to be absolute certainty of survival. Unfortunately, that is not the case.

I watch my hand sign the form. I am detached. There is a sickening feeling in my stomach. I have become nauseated. Before I have completed my signature, tears have welled up in my eyes and I can barely make out the tail end of my signature.

We both dread the moment of realization at the signing of the form.

We hug and kiss our baby. He does not fully understand what is going on. We have to be strong and act like what is about to happen is small and meaningless. We don't want him to know we are worried sick. We don't want him to sense weakness. We want him to feel he will see us in a few simple moments and that nothing will prevent this inevitability.

The nurse takes our baby. Our baby is crying about his separation from Mommy and Daddy and he is in the arms of a stranger. The nurse turns and walks away with him in her arms. My wife and I hug each other and cry.

I say prayers. God, take care of my baby. Please don't let anything happen to him. God, please listen to me. Let him be strong. Andrew, you be strong; God let him be strong. Andrew you have to be strong. You have to be strong for Mommy and Daddy.

There is no happiness, there is no feeling, there is no refreshing breath, there is no life in us until the moment our son is wheeled out of the operating room surrounded and followed by his teams of doctors. We will stay bedside until he is well.

We as parents realize that we are not the ones who suffer the most behind these ordeals. Clearly, our suffering is not as great as theirs.

We want each of our boys to live as normal a life as possible and we have done everything within our power to insure that they do. However, we have spoiled them. And, we have done so purposefully.

Recently, we had a very good family friend join us for dinner. He said he had noticed that our boys were staying up a little late and they seem to get away with things which would have brought his mother's wrath upon him had he done these things as a child. He went on to state that other of our common friends had commented to him that they had noticed the same things with reference to our sons.

Our response, although generated by anger at first, was completed behind tears. People do not realize what these boys are going to go through. They do not understand that these boys are facing at least one and very possibly more than one open-heart surgery. That in their future, they each will face the moment they are wheeled away from their mother and father with the knowledge that people they do not know are going to be opening their chest to work on the beating core of their existence. They will be removed from the only comfort they know into the terrible horror of the foreign operating room and the unfamiliar faces. I cannot imagine but that they will be crying at that moment. They will be agonizing. They will be scared beyond our comprehension. And if they are old enough to understand by that time, they will have heard their Mom and Dad repeat over and over again that they are very strong and that God is going to take care of them. They will have heard that they will be awakened in another room with Mom and Dad at their side in just a little while. And they will see Mommy and Daddy acting very strong, like it's no big deal. We don't want them to see us cry or to see us weak or worried. But we know that it is a big deal. And we know that to them it will be a big deal.

When it comes to our sons, we don't care what our friends think. We are going to spoil them. The ordeals our boys face are overwhelming. Our sons are the most precious, special boys in the world and they deserve to be spoiled. They deserve to enjoy their lives to the fullest because their futures are uncertain and to an extent, frightening.

Our friend seemed sympathetic and understanding. He confessed he believed our sons health problems had been cured and he had not known what lies ahead.

We dread those future moments as the dates for surgery approach. We know they are ahead of us getting closer day by day. When we stop to think about it, as unfortunately we do quite often, we cry.

Our boys are growing up too quickly. They are getting big. These thoughts make us cry too.

We know that as time goes on, we are getting closer to the moment when we must again sign the next informed consent form and watch as the nurse turns around with our son in her arms. We will watch her carry him or roll him down the hall until we cannot see them any more. And then we will hold each other and cry.

Believe us, we have learned to cherish, really cherish, every moment with our sons.

A few years back, a friend requested that our family join him and his daughter in presenting his company's donation to the Children's Miracle Network during the telethon. That was the beginning of a wonderful relationship with an awesome organization and its members from our Children's Hospital in Los Angeles.

There are not enough words to describe how special CMN and our CHLA Foundations are and how special they make us and our children feel. Through the events sponsored by CMN, we have been fortunate to meet other families in our situation with children facing challenges.

Andy, through you we would like to tell other families that if they suspect there is something wrong with their child, or they know something is wrong and they have not gone to [their] Children's Hospital, they should GO. Children's Hospital and CMN are dedicated to take care of our little babies. They specialize in little hearts, little bones, little lungs, etc. They do not treat adults unless they have treated them as children. It takes very specialized doctors to take care of our little ones.

You know, our oldest son Brandon recently broke his arm. We immediately took him to the emergency room that was 5 minutes away from our house. CHLA is at least 30 to 45 minutes away. We spent over 21/2 hours at the local hospital. They treated us rudely, placed us in a room where the police had an adult male in custody, and they ignored us. Worst of all, they sent Brandon home with a bucal fracture of the ulnar bones without a cast because the doctor was not sure if there was a fracture. The doctor on duty admitted he could not read the [child's] x-ray.

The following morning, we took Brandon to CHLA where they immediately diagnosed the fractures and placed his arm in a cast. If we had gone to CHLA in the first place, Brandon would not have suffered in pain for those additional hours. Obviously, our local community hospital is not trained in little bones - little people.

There is a reason why Children's Hospitals exist. And there is a reason why CMN exists. With CMN's efforts, the hospitals are receiving funding to continue their expertise in our little ones.

Thank you Children's Miracle Network. Thank you Children's Hospital Los Angeles. And thank you to all the rest of the Children's Hospitals for your sincere dedication and devotion to our children. You have made and continue to make a difference in our lives.

Sincerely yours,

Alan + Rita

Alan and Rita Shapiro

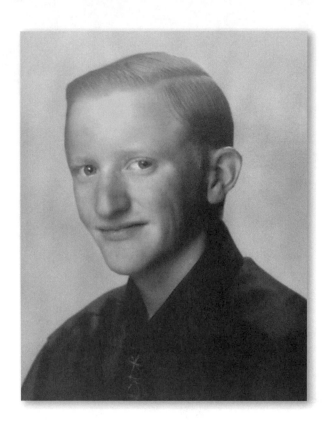

...he participates in numerous activities and he is on the advanced education program at his school.

Sam Lowry

Sam is not a doctor. He doesn't even play one on TV! But he did accurately diagnose himself and report his findings to the real medical professionals. Toward the end of 1995, Sam's weight dropped, he developed an unquenchable thirst and urinated more frequently than normal. He also experienced extreme fatigue.

After consulting a computer encyclopedia, Sam discovered that he had four of the five major symptoms of diabetes. He approached his mother with his concern and his parents took him to a doctor who confirmed Sam's suspicions. He was immediately admitted to Memorial Medical Center in Las Cruces, New Mexico with a blood sugar count of over 500.

As you read Sam's letter, take note of the incredible attitude he displays. This guy is a world changer. When I am tempted to let truly small things ruin my day, I will remember Sam's comment about lemons. Read on!

SAM LOWRY

Mr. Andy Andrews
P.O. Box 2761
Gulf Shores, Alabama 36547

Dear Andy,

Thank you Andy for asking me to be a part of this important project. I am fifteen and have had type one diabetes for three years. My family and I were overwhelmed when I was diagnosed on December 26, 1995. No one in our family has ever had type one diabetes and we didn't know much about diabetes in general. I hadn't been feeling well for a few months and was always thirsty. Thirst was the only symptom of diabetes we were familiar with and when I looked up diabetes on our computer encyclopedia I found I had several of the major symptoms of juvenile diabetes. Because we had no family history of the disease my folks didn't think that could be it, but when I didn't start feeling better, it was time to find out what was happening.

At first I was terrified just like any other twelve year old would have been considering all of the blood tests that I underwent not to mention discovering the fact that diabetes is a life long disease. Injecting insulin several times daily is the only treatment for juvenile diabetes since the pancreas gradually quits producing insulin on its own. After the initial shock had worn off and once my family was around me in the hospital, I sat back and had a little conversation with myself about what was going to happen to me.

Developing diabetes in the early to mid 1900's meant that the person who acquired it was probably fated to die a miserable death. But in the late 1990's thanks to modern medicine and technology, people with diabetes are able to live long and healthy lives. After realizing this I decided I was not going to "give in" to something that was a manageable disease. I decided that developing diabetes is just one one of those metaphorical "lemons" that life has handed me, but that with the proper knowledge of my condition, as well as the right mind set that I was not only going to make lemonade but that I was going to make lemon pie too!

After living with diabetes for three years I have had to make some changes in my overall lifestyle. Other than the required monitoring of my blood glucose levels several times a day, injecting insulin before meals, and having to carefully plan meals, I have not had to slow down one bit. Sure, it was difficult to adjust at first but I have found that doing these things on a daily basis has become more of a habit. A habit that is a "pain in the neck" of course, but it is better than the alternative.

Andy, I would like to take time to thank the people that have helped me from day one since being diagnosed with diabetes. First of all, I would like to thank my endocrinologist, Dr. Ellen Kaufman as well as her great staff.   In addition, I would like to thank Lola Cunico, diabetes educator, and the staff at Memorial Medical Center in Las Cruces, New Mexico. I would also like to thank my entire family, the driving force behind my goal to be healthy and continue to live life to the fullest. To Mom and Dad, Amanda and Trey, all of my aunts, uncles, cousins and grandparents - thank you for all of your love and support. And last but not least, I would like to send a big thank you out to all of the people who give so much time, and devote many hours of hard work to the Children's Miracle Network. Each of you have a special place in my heart. Thanks again! I hope to see you all sometime down the road.

And to all of you that are facing challenges of any sort, medical or otherwise, I have only a few pieces of advice to give to you. Don't give up, live life to its fullest, and perhaps one of the most important things and yet one often overlooked, the ability to "keep smiling" even when things get tough. Take the time to relax and have a good laugh. Even if time does not permit and all you have is but a moment away from the toils of everyday life, that's all it takes; just a moment to smile and be happy!

Thanks again Andy
Sincerely,

Sam Lowry

"Do not pray for easy lives. Pray to be stronger men. Do not pray for tasks equal to your powers. Pray for powers equal to your tasks! Then the doing of your work shall be no miracle, but you shall be a miracle. Every day you will wonder at yourself, at the richness of life that has come to you by the Grace of God."

– Philip Brooks

FUTURE SPECIAL NEEDS TEACHER

...when he grows up he wants to be a Special Needs (Inclusion) Teacher at the elementary level. Enjoys working with children and would like to help children who need more care and love.

Mark Coley

Mark was diagnosed with Crohn's Disease in September 1998. Crohn's Disease is an inflammatory disease of the digestive tract. In Mark's case, his large and small intestines became blocked. After several months of intense drug and diet therapy, Mark had made no progress. His weight was down to 66 pounds and it became necessary for him to receive nutrition through a central line catheter.

Soon, doctors decided to remove several inches of Mark's large and small intestines. He was released from the hospital one week later and has been on an upswing ever since. Mark will always fight Crohn's Disease and presently takes medication to prevent another episode. Today, Mark's weight is normal, his attitude is exceptional, and his future is unlimited.

Mr. Andy Andrews
P.O. Box 3709
Gulf Shores, AL 36547

Dear Andy:

I am honored to have the opportunity to write a letter for your book. This year has been full of surprises for me. After being chosen to represent Arizona at the CMN telethon, I am happy to be a part of your book about kids like me.

 When school started last year, I did not feel very well. My stomach hurt almost all the time. My parents told me it was because I was nervous about school starting, so I just tried to make it through the days. After the first few weeks of school, I got very sick and missed a week of school. My parents and the doctors said it was the flu. Several weeks later, I had to be rushed to the emergency room because of the pains I was having. I hurt so much that I could not walk. The doctors told me I had appendicitis. I was very worried and scared. I was admitted to the hospital and the doctors decided that I had Crohn's Disease. I was afraid of this disease because I had never heard of it. I wish it had been appendicitis because I would have gotten well quicker. After a week in the hospital, they gave me many medicines and a strict diet to cure my Crohn's. It was hard getting used to taking so many pills. Around Thanksgiving, we found out that the medicine was not working and I needed surgery. In December, I had part of my intestines removed. I went home three days before Christmas and enjoyed the best holiday ever.

Before I knew I had Crohn's, it was hard because my parents and teachers thought I was faking it. I felt different because I was smaller than the rest of the kids in my class. I did not like being sick all the time and I could not understand what was happening to me.

After my diagnosis, I felt very lonely. I did not think anyone knew my feelings. My friends did not really understand what was happening to me and they asked a lot of questions. Some of them thought they would "catch" the disease from me. Some of them thought that I would die. They made me feel different. Being sick has taught me to appreciate my friends. It also has made me a little more popular.

Crohn's disease will be a part of my life forever. I will always have to take medications and be on a special diet. If I am lucky, I will never have surgery again. It is hard for me to understand why I am sick. The doctors say it is a genetic disease, but I am the only person in my family with it. I have learned to live each day to the fullest and appreciate the happy/healthy times.

After going to the CMN Telethon, I know that I am not alone. I have met many other kids who have more challenges than me. They are my new friends. We can all face our challenges in life together. I wish to thank CMN for all the wonderful miracles they worked for my family and other kids like me.

My advice to other kids facing serious illnesses is to hang on because your miracle will come soon. Until then, stay positive and live your life to the fullest.

Your New Pal,

MARK COLEY

"The best and most beautiful things in the world cannot be seen or even touched. They must be felt with the heart."

– Helen Keller

ENJOYS COUNTRY MUSIC

...loves people and talking with her best friend. She is going to make a difference in this world.

Stacey Smith

Look at her picture. Stacey is quite obviously a gorgeous young woman on the outside. Her heart and spirit, however, are many times more beautiful. I have heard the saying, ""To whom much is given, much is expected." But I never considered the application of this truth to someone like Stacey.

My wife and I read Stacey's letter together and shook our heads in wonder and disgust over the letter she was sent by an anonymous person. Can God use angels like Stacey to educate and enlighten the rest of us? I believe it is not only possible but probable. Stacey's gift was an incurable disease with a horrendous social stigma. What is expected of her? Many would answer: nothing. But, of course, Stacy knows that God expects her best, and she is giving it. Stacey Smith is in the forefront of a fight for understanding and compassion. She is not fighting for herself, but for the unfortunate multitude who do not possess her faith and strength.

Stacey Renee Smith

1502 Stacey Lane ~ Annapolis, Maryland, 21404 ~ USA

Andy Andrews
P.O. Box 2761
Gulf Shores, AL., 36547

Dear Andy,

When I received your letter requesting a letter from me, I was first overly excited then confused as to how in one letter I could make an impact on someone's life. Then as I read through your books I realized how impacted I was. I am not famous or rich, I am a seventeen year old girl who is HIV+.

My name is Stacey Smith. I received a blood transfusion when I was 2 years old and contracted this awful virus. My life has been turned upside down due to this virus. I have been in and out of hospitals all my life and don't ever remember being "normal". I was an innocent bystander who needed a blood transfusion to save my life and it did that, but 4 years later I was sick again and was told I was HIV+.

HIV has changed my life in more ways then I can count, I have lost friends, I have been harassed at school and received letters saying "Take your AIDS infested body and get out now", I have never been able to keep up in school. I am always getting a cold or other illness and missing two weeks at a time. HIV has left it's marks on my family also. It has been very hard for everyone who loves me. Waking up each morning and looking in the mirror has become a task I have been very depressed to the point I have tried killing myself.

HIV has played a large part in my life but I still continue to live because I have learned many things from it. You'll never realize how important it is to live each day to the fullest and never take one second for granted until you are looked at by a doctor and told you are going to die! I would have never had the things I have now if it weren't for HIV. People forget to say they love you or care because they are sure they will see you again but living with a virus that has no rules makes me understand that my life could end and I must be ready for that. I never leave a room without saying "I love you" or "goodbye" because life is short and I have a need to tell people how much they mean to me before I never have a chance to! Being HIV+ for 15 years makes me realize how important the little things are and how lucky I am to be alive!

I have been lucky to have a team of doctors, an extraordinary hospital and the love and support of my family and friends. I am lucky enough to go to John's Hopkins Hospital one of the best Children's hospitals in the world. I am also lucky to be a Children's Miracle Network Champion! I was given a trip to Florida and Washington D.C. The people who make that possible like IOF and Disney World have no clue what it means to a kid to be giving something back for being sick all of their life! To everyone that played a part in the 1999 telethon thank you for allowing me to be a part of it from the bottom of my heart!

I will be a senior in high school this year, and if all goes well I will graduate in the year 2000. I am doing very well right now, I haven't been really sick in a few months! To everyone that is sick with any kind of illness. I would say fight it put every ounce of you mind, body ,and soul in to it! You can make it. I have survived against all odds, I will keep fighting until it is time to take my place in heaven.

Look to God for strength and courage and you will be ok! I can not take away the pain from you or make the feeling change. I can tell you that in the last several months I have turned to God to be my strength and I am much happier and more at peace. Give your problems to God and he will be you best friend. When you feel no one else understands. If you give your heart to him and trust in him you will never go through the pain alone!

Here is a poem I wrote about living with AIDS and knowing No one can understand fully what it is to be robbed of you life at a young age.

Do you really Know?
Do you know how hard it is to hold my head up high?
Do you know how hard it is to not break down and cry?

Do you how hard it is to calm my childish fears?
Do you know how hard it is to wipe away my tears?

Do you know how hard it is to brush my life aside?
Do you know how hard it is to hold it all inside?

Do you know how hard it is to listen to the hate?
Do you know how hard it is to meet a person who can relate?

Do you really Know how hard it is to just live my life?
If you don't, then count your blessings, but to those who do, never stop wishing.

Make the best of what you have and keep going strong! Life is hard but we must keep going, there are to many important things we need to do! Always Smile and never be afraid to reach out for a friend! Even when there is no light at the end of the tunnel keep searching. It is there! There is always HOPE! God is always with you. Look to him for the answers. Thank you for listening. God bless you always!

Love always,

Stacey Renee Smith
Stacey Renee Smith

"You can't be brave if you've only had wonderful things happen to you."

– Mary Tyler Moore

Wes and Regina

Kaci

THIS FAMILY LOVES TO READ AND TRAVEL

Regina enjoys cooking and Wes and Kaci enjoy eating. They are a great family and believe they would not have survived this ordeal without each other and their faith in God.

The Caves Family

Kaci has a beautiful smile. As I read these letters from Kaci and her mother, Regina, I was moved by her ability to let us see it. Kaci is simply a remarkable young woman. Not because of what she has been through, but who she has become in spite of the challenges she has faced.

The whole ordeal may have actually been harder for Regina. As a parent, I can imagine the feelings of helplessness that must have enveloped Regina and her husband, Wes, as they watched their only daughter in a fight for her life.

This is a very special family. They are active in their church and other volunteer efforts. Wes and Regina celebrate 25 years of marriage soon and look forward to watching Kaci grow up. Kaci would like to one day be a fashion designer.

Dear Mr. Andrews,

Thank you so much for the chance to help others through your book. I believe there are many people who have lived their lives with problems, and I am just one of the many that have challenges. Seeing the other forty-nine champions during the 1998 CMN convention showed me that.

I did have one-half of my brain removed in 1996, but I believe it was no big deal. I am who I am and I feel very thankful that I am alive. I don't feel any different than any other person; I just have to do it slower and maybe a little differently with some adaptations.

My life from 1993 to 1996 was almost completely made up of trying different medication, hospitals, and hundreds of seizures a day. After my left hemispherectomy surgery, my life was full of rehabilitation for months and it is still ongoing. But you know what? I'm alive and I feel blessed by the Lord for letting me go on. My advice to others is have faith, never give up, and work hard.

There are many problems I must deal with daily, but with God's help and the support of my family and friends I will make it and do it to the best of my ability.

I hope my challenge is an example to others that you never take life for granted and you give 100% everyday to make your world and the world of those around you a better place.

Keep the faith,

Kaci

Kaci Caves

Dear Mr. Andrews,

We would like to thank you for the opportunity to share our experience with others during our trials with our daughter Kaci and her amazing ability to overcome her illness. No parent ever thinks they will have to face the choices we were faced with, but when it happens you realize the strength that your faith gives you to cope and go forward.

A single seizure on that night in May of 1993 changed our lives forever. The seizure led to a degenerative brain disease that could cause death or must be cured by an operation that requires removal of half the brain. Through the next three and a half years we tried a variety of drugs, medical treatments that were experimental, special diets, but mostly a lot of prayers. In the end the disease took over and our only option was the operation--a hemispherectomy.

By the fall of 1996, our daughter was almost 14 years old, she was having seizures non-stop, was in a wheelchair, making trips to the hospital every eight weeks, taking 40 to 50 pills a day, and was totally dependent on her parents for help with her everyday needs. Her quality of life had reached a point where she barely existed. She was being taught homebound and was so lethargic because of the drugs that she slept a great deal of the time. It was time to make a decision and the only one we could make was to allow the surgery to be scheduled.

How do you let them take her away for this type of surgery? The answer is only with a lot of faith, many prayers, and believing God will allow this child to live.

Kaci's life after surgery has been so full of rehabilitation and struggles, but you go forward because she has the strength and stamina to keep you motivated and heading in the right direction.

At 14, she had to relearn a great deal of her language, how to read again besides learning to walk and live with the right half of her body paralyzed. It was easier for us than most because she did it daily with a great big smile and a heart full of determination. Even when your heart as a parent is breaking as you see all of your dreams for this child shattered, you go on with your life and make the very best out of it because you know you are blessed to have had this wonderful child.

Through this experience, you realize that life is so precious and you must take each problem one day at a time. We have developed such a different outlook on life as we watch Kaci learn to live her life with half a brain. Her optimism for her future is contagious so you grab hold of her dreams and make plans for a life that is so full and rich and enjoy the trip along the way thanking God daily for the life he has given each of us.

Sincerely,

Wes and Regina Caves

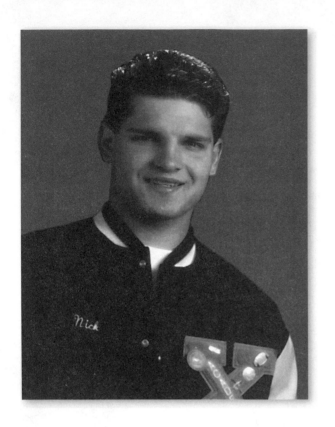

CHAMPION AMONG CHAMPIONS

...his life is full of love, sports, girls, school and music. His lifetime goal is to be a professional baseball player.

Nicholas Olszewski

The day Nick was born, his grandfather wrote a letter to him, telling him how much he loved him, how much he looked forward to teaching him how to throw a ball, and how much he wanted to see him grow up into a good and caring man. Then, the grandfather wrote the baby's obituary. "I had to do it," he said. "The doctors gave us so little hope." And yet, he could see the fight in his eyes. "I know it's difficult to believe about a three pound baby, but the fight was there."

After 48 surgeries, Nick has now lettered in baseball, basketball, and football. He is an honor student at Marquette University, writes poetry, and loves the theater. Nick has also shaken hands with the President of the United States. His grandfather's obituary, it seems, was far too premature.

Nicholas Olszewski

Mr. Andy Andrews
P.O. 3709
Gulf Shores, Alabama 36547

Dear Andy,

On December 11, 1979, my mother gave birth to me in Appleton, Wisconsin. I was born 4 weeks premature, weighed less than 4 pounds and given very little chance of survival. "I don't want to paint you a rosy picture" are the words the doctors told my parents and my grandparents of my chance of living, for I was born with numerous birth defects and not supposed to make through the first day of my life. I am glad I was not able to hear the doctor speak those words, because I might have believed him and given up on life and died. Shortly after my birth they transported me to Children's Hospital of Wisconsin, and that is where my long journey began.

Transposition of the great vessels, tethered spinal cord, imperferated anus, T.E. Fistula. Words my parents never dreamed of hearing were now their reality, and what would consume there lives for the next 19 years. True, my 19 years on this earth were not always "rosy". But whose life really is? I have undergone 48 surgeries and hundreds of other procedures at Children's Hospital of Wisconsin, and thanks to the Children's Hospital, I am now able to attend Marquette University, and have participated in all sports, theater, and have been a honor student all through school. True my life has never been a normal life, it was always interrupted by health problems. But it has been a bitter sweet 19 years, and now I am in a position to help other children who are going through the same emotional and physical pain I did.

Growing up with my problems made me realize how many wonderful and talented people there are. I have attained a sense of love and appreciation for my family, friends, and doctors few people will ever realize. They were always there for me with so much love and support. I have acquired a deep appreciation for every day, and every opportunity that occurs in my daily life. It may be a cliché but I really feel "there is no day like today".

There were days when love and emotional support were not enough and I needed more extensive care, and for all those times I am so grateful for the staff at Children's Hospital. Their skill and knowledge of a child's mind and body have made it possible for me and other children to live. Now being 19 and STILL being a patient there, I have the opportunity to return something to the hospital by giving testimonial speeches at there fund raisers, and co-hosting our local Children's Miracle Network Telethon.

Andy, many people have asked me how I have survived these trying times. My answer has always been, you must concentrate on the things and people you love. Never dwell on your problems and how bad you feel at that time in your life. The situation will improve. You will feel better again, and someday soon your life will return back to normal. Thank God for every day you have been given, and paint your own rosy picture.

Sincerely,

Nicholas J. Olszewski

ENTERTAINER

...got the acting bug when he was eight years old and has not slowed down ever since. He is a multi-talented performer with credits spanning television, theatre and music.

John R. Schneider

I first met John at a taping of a TNN show several years ago. His warmth and genuine spirit was instantly apparent, and I liked him immediately. He laughs easily and is not "taken with himself" as so many entertainers are. His credits, however, are impressive.

Audiences best know John for his role as Bo Duke on the popular television series "The Dukes of Hazzard". He was also a regular on "Dr. Quinn, Medicine Woman" and stars in the Nickelodeon movie "Snow Day". A respected singer/songwriter, John did 487 performances of the Tony award winning musical, "Grand Hotel", and has eleven solo albums. These include a number one album and four number one singles.

Recognizing the need for better health care for children, John co-founded the Children's Miracle Network. I'm certain you will enjoy John's letter about his friend!

Andy Andrews
P.O. Box 2761
Gulf Shores, AL 36547

FROM THE DESK OF

JOHN R. SCHNEIDER

Andy,

I wanted to take a moment to tell you about a miracle of HUGE proportions!
I know that you are in to the miraculous so... here goes!

What seems like a short while ago (actually it was almost 20 years ago!) a
couple of friends of mine and I found out about someone, let's call this
someone Gus, that was sick and not doing very well. Well... after working
with Gus for two years we decided that we needed to get him out of his
present environment and into a new atmosphere. This wasn't going to be
easy because the folks where he was staying really didn't want him to go
and seemed happy with his condition. They had grown to accept his current
condition as the "best he could hope for."

Not good enough! Where a child's health is being considered why settle for
"okay" when you can have "great!"

Anyway... the four of us took the Gus away from where he was and began
the task of convincing others to take him on as a hopeful patient. It took
most of a year to get Gus placed in another situation because most everyone
in the country agreed with the prior prognosis. EVERYONE said that we
should leave well enough alone.

Being the stubborn, dreamers that we were and still are, we kept looking and
finally found a group in Chicago that agreed to give Gus a try! We were
ecstatic and so was Gus!!

It gets better!!

Soon after treatment started for Gus we all realized that there were going to
be tremendous on-going expenses for Gus and that we just didn't have it!
Well... twelve hours into Gus's first major operation a philanthropic
company stepped in and announced that they would be happy to underwrite
the next operation if need be.

Okay... maybe you've caught on to my story here. I'm actually not talking
about a person here at all but an annual event that has definitely changed

many lives in the eighteen years since its inception. I'm talking about The children's Miracle Network! CMN started from an idea whose time had come and whose early supporters just didn't want to let fall through the cracks.

With the determination and, yes, stubbornness of everyone involved, CMN survived a very shaky beginning and each of it's annual "operations" or "broadcasts" to become the single largest fund raising effort of its kind in the world today! A true testimony of why everyone everywhere should follow their dreams and "go for it"!

With over ONE AND ONE HALF BILLION dollars raised so far, all of which has gone to those who need it most, the children, I can say with both volume and pride that the "operation" has been a success!

Follow your dreams!

Sincerely,

John R. Schneider

"I thank God for my handicaps, for through them I have found myself, my work and my God."

– Helen Keller

...her favorite sport is volleyball and would love to play in Jamaica. If she could invent a food it would be coffee. It would have almond, French vanilla, mocha and eight shots of espresso. She would call it a "Hot Rush."

Nikki Anderson

If Nikki could go back to any time in which to live, she says she'd be a part of the sixties. She would love to live when Janis Joplin did. Nikki has a burn to sing like Joplin or her current favorite, Alanis Morissette. She is interested in yoga, biking, gardening, and doing anything with animals. Nikki wants to learn how to treat people and animals with muscle injuries. Her dream horse would be a Lippizaner, but would settle for a Palomino or Quarter horse.

Nikki enjoys hearing her dad play the electric guitar. She says her dad is awesome, but that the guitar needs to be tuned! She beats her mom at Backgammon and will play Monopoly or spoons with anyone who is up to the challenge. I see Nikki as a young lady who would be hard to beat in almost any contest. She has already beaten one major foe in her life. She can take all comers!

Nikki Anderson

my story

Hi. My name is Nikki Anderson. I am 16 years old, and I was in a car accident when I was 12. I suffered a traumatic brain injury, or TBI. I have a long story to tell about my injury, but there are other miracles that need to be told, so I'll try and keep this one short. The shorter version of my story goes like this:

I got out of school June 8 for summer vacation. I left the following weekend to North Dakota with my aunt Steph and her boyfriend Ian for two weeks. Everything was great; I've loved animals my whole life (especially horses) and I was with animals my whole stay, Steph and I went moonlight riding every night, with me riding my favorite horse Callie, and her on the hot lady, CC. We went fishing at a nearby trout pond with one of her next-door neighbors boys, James. James and I also went horseback-riding together. His Mom worked at the local zoo, so Steph brought me there, too.

Ian was a vet and worked at the clinic in town, so I went there alot, and saw all the animals in need. Watching him give them shots and stuff made my knees a little weak, though. That experience changed my future career plans.

Every morning after I got up, I went out to the barn to collect chicken eggs and feed the horses. One morning after I got the eggs, I walked over to get the grain, and then opened the bin to feed the horses, and inside were the cutest baby kittens that I'd ever seen! There were 7 if I can remember.
Just before I went moonlight-riding later that week, around 3 days before I had to go, I called my Dad to see if I could stay longer. I told him I was having *the best-time*. He said yes I could.

So I stayed, and a couple days later we were all invited to a picnic in Fargo. The morning of the picnic, Steph was running behind as usual, so Ian was supposed to drive me, and Steph would meet us up there.

So Ian and I got in the car to go, (he thought he saw me put my seatbelt on) and we went. Around half way there, on a highway, there was a dirt road with a stop sign on my right. I was riding in the passengers side, and Ian had asked me to get something off the floor. To do that I had to take off my seatbelt. It must have been the wrong timing, because as I looked up to see what was coming, and we got hit.

My forehead went thru the windshield, and my head got all beat up. Ian wasn't wearing a seatbelt either, but he had an air bag. He hurt his knee pretty bad, but he still crawled over what was left of the car and found me unconscious and gave me CPR. That got me breathing again, but I was still unconscious.

-God bless the person that reported the accident, because I would be six feet under if they hadn't!-

I was immediately ambulanced to the hospital in Whapeton for less than an hour, then air lifted to MeritCare in Fargo for 10 days, where they had to put a monitoring device on my head, and then transported to Gillette Children's Hospital in St. Paul where I stayed for over 20 (long) weeks, 13 of which I was in my coma.

The doctors told my parents that I was in a level 4 coma. The coma levels range 1 through 5, and 5 is brain-dead. I also had a broken collar bone and a broken femur.

A close friend of mine wrote a letter to the St. Paul Chief of Police asking him to come with his horses and visit me a few times at the hospital. The police were so touched by this letter that they came almost every week, and not too long later, I started responding.

My aunt Stephanie brought my favorite horse Callie to Gillette many times to visit me. One special time, Steph brought Callie into the parking lot, and Callie was nuzzling my face, and I reacted, and Steph said, "She's yours now, Nikki."

They put a feeding tube in my nose, and later replaced that with a tube in my belly, which I later named Bob, casts on my legs to straighten out my stiffened feet, and a metal plate in my leg to fix my femur.

I became clinically conscious in August, and went through long days of speech, physical, occupational, and psychological therapy, along with educational. My Dad and sister came every day right after work and school and stayed by me all night, my Mom brought my dog Maggie to sleep with me many nights after work, even after visiting hours, my Grandma and Grandpa came every day, my Grandma on the other side of the family came when she could, and my Grandpa on my Mom's side of the family came whenever he could. Occasionally I got visits from out of town.

The day I was released, October 13, which happened to be a Friday, my step-Grandma rented me a limousine to ride home in with my Dad and 3 friends! We got to drink non- alcoholic champagne, and when we got home, I was welcomed with a red carpet! Callie came home with me, and stayed in my back yard, over night!!!

In '96 I had the best time of my life at Alanis Morissette's concert!!!

I was pretty popular before my accident, I was famous after it, and all my friends stuck with me through it, but now they're all gone. Just acquaintances in the halls at school.

This year (1999), I have improved alot, although I don't see it because I live with it. I have never liked school, and I still don't. I'm not getting the best grades, and I wish I could do better. (especially Math and English) But I try, and that's the best anyone can do.

At this point in my life, my dream is to be a singer like Janis Joplin was and Alanis Morissette is, (my two all-time fav's) but I don't have a voice and I really need lessons; my first career choice is a Vet-Tech, second is a Physical Therapist, and third is a Florist. I want to marry and have 5 children; live in a big house with a spiral staircase and walk-in closet in my room; own my own humane society, and have a purplish-brown BMW Z3 turbo, and/or a Porsche just like Janis Joplin's to call my own. I might be a little over-wishful, but hey, everyone has to dream.

Thank you to everyone who stood by me through this hellish experience, my Physical Therapists, and everyone who helped me pull through, you know who you are. I love you Mom, Dad and Kirstin!!!

Nikki J. Anderson

Cindy and Ernie

LOVES THE OUTDOORS

...they endured many hardships, but this a family of fighters and survivors. Their son has taught them to have a positive outlook and that blessings are disguised in many ways.

Ernie and Cindy Long

Ernie was a country boy raised on a small farm in North Dakota. Cindy was a city girl who grew up in the suburbs of Minneapolis. They met as adults working different shifts at the same factory. Their schedule made for a unique dating experience, but love (and the lack of sleep) won out and they were married in February of 1973.

Ernie now works at the aluminum factory in nearby Columbia Falls while Cindy spends her days as a nursing assistant. They love to camp and fish with their family and do so quite often. Ernie and Cindy have four sons, the youngest of whom is Ethan. Cindy says, "He turned our lives upside down for a while, but he has been such a blessing. Ethan smiles from the time he gets up in the morning until bedtime at night."

$$\mathscr{ELC}$$

Ernie and Cindy Long

Andy
P.O. Box 3709
Gulf Shores, AL
36547

Dear Andy,

   Ethan was born on April 19th 1989 and was found to have a heart murmur that when investigated indicated he needed to be airlifted to Children's hospital in Seattle Washington. They told us he had aortic stenosis and coarctation of the aorta. The doctors watched him for a few days deciding on the course they were going to take. One week from his birth he had a catherization and went into coarctation repair surgery the next morning with the hope that with this surgery Ethan would be able to go home and grow. Ethan didn't get to go home at that time as hoped. Two weeks after his first surgery Ethan went into congestive heart failure. Two days later Ethan had to have open heart surgery. The surgeon performed an aortic valvulotomy, opening his aortic valve up some, in the hope that this would give Ethan a little more time. The surgeon didn't give us much hope that Ethan would survive this operation, but the option was to do nothing. Ethan surprised everyone and came through the operation with no problems. Ethan got to come home just before he turned six weeks old. His doctors hoped that he would make it to the age of two or better with the surgery that they performed, that would make Ethan big enough for an artificial valve. Actually, the doctors didn't expect to ever see Ethan again. He surprised them again and at the age of 17 months he was on his way back to Children's. Seattle had gotten the approval from the FDA to try a very small valve that they had gotten three of. In September of 1990 he first went in for another catherization which didn't go very well. Ethan had a severe reaction to the dye and they almost lost him. He made it threw with only a very swollen eye lid to show for it but it looked pretty rough. The next day Ethan was scheduled for valve replacement surgery with once again very slim odds. That to us was our worst experience. At 17 months old they don't understand why people are doing all these things to them and especially why the people you trust, your parents, are letting them do this to you. Ethan lost his trust in us and he give us the purest look of hatred we've ever seen as his last look before he went into surgery. Knowing that Ethan didn't understand why we would allow this to happen to him didn't make things any easier for us. Thankfully, he once again beat the odds that the doctors gave him. After days of his not looking at us or letting us touch him he grabbed hold of mom's finger and held on as tight as he could and wouldn't let go. Ethan had been given an external pacemaker at the time of surgery and not long after surgery there was some problem so he went back into surgery to get a permanent pacemaker implanted. He was diagnosed with total heart block and will always need a pacemaker. The next couple of years were spent on trips for check ups and tests. In 1993 the first surgery that Ethan has some memories of was for a new pacemaker. We made annual trips to Seattle until 1997. The doctors were amazed at how well this small valve was working for such a long time.
   1996 was a big year for Ethan. Ethan was Montana's representative for the Children's Miracle Network, so Ethan got a trip to Washington D.C. and Disney World. You had to have been here to know what that meant to Ethan. He sang songs about how lucky he was to get to go from the time he got up while dancing around the house for days and days. Ethan was in the news and in the paper so he thought he was the luckiest person alive.
   Last year in 1998 we had our biggest scare we've had in a long time. We had taken Ethan to North Dakota for a fishing trip with grandpa before going to Seattle in June for his valve replacement surgery. We only got one pole in the river when Ethan fainted. We recognized this as a pacemaker problem and took Ethan to the emergency room at Williston. The facility at Williston couldn't handle this problem, so

they called for an air ambulance to Bismark. Amazingly, his pacemaker worked all the way to Bismark and through the night. It quit working at 5:30am the next morning. Ethan boarded another air ambulance for a trip to Minneapolis. This trip his pacemaker didn't work, but he was stable and he talked the ears off the nurse and doctor in the back of the plane. At one time from all the medication he'd gotten to help him relax he dozed off. The doctor and nurse tried to wake him and he didn't respond so the doctor gave him a jolt from the external pacemaker that he was hooked up to. He responded with "DON'T YOU DARE DO THAT AGAIN" I'm just taking a nap. Ethan arrived at the airport and was transferred to a ground ambulance which took him to Minneapolis Children's Hospital. At arrival at the hospital his heart had stopped and the doctors were giving him CPR. The doctors got Ethan in the hospital where they inserted a pacer line up through the groin and hooked him up to an external pacer. This procedure give the doctors time to get Ethan into surgery and install a new pacemaker and wires. After the surgery the doctors told us that one of the wires from the pacemaker to the heart had broken and wasn't getting connected to the heart. It was at this time that the doctors told us that Ethan was ready for a new valve. The pressures in the heart chamber were getting very high. The doctors told us about a procedure that they do called the "Ross procedure". This procedure uses your own pulmonary valve in the aortic area and uses a cadaver valve in the pulmonary area. The reason behind this procedure is the pulmonary valve is much easier to get to. The doctors hope to never have to deal with the aortic valve again and the patient would no longer need to be on blood thinners. Unfortunately this doesn't eliminate any further surgery and the pulmonary doesn't grow with you and will need changing at some point. This valve is easier and less dangerous to get to so that is why they prefer this choice. We spent the next three months back in Montana, having fun, camping, fishing and researching "the Ross procedure". After much thought, we chose "the Ross". In September we returned to Minneapolis to have Ethan's surgery. It was a very difficult time for all of us. Ethan was old enough that he understood what was going to happen, but never the less he still was scared. Ethan's mom got to go into the operating room and hold his hand until the doctors put him under. The surgery lasted seven hours, at one point the cardiologist come to tell us that the doctors didn't think that they would be able to continue with "the Ross". Ethan had so much scar tissue that was bound together in the area of the pulmonary valve. The doctors kept trying and were able to accomplish it. The surgeon told us that this was the most difficult operation that they had done and was amazed that they were able to accomplish it. Ethan is now also totally dependent on his pacemaker for his ventricular beat, but is getting ready to turn 10 in April. He is as active and healthy looking as the next kid. Without friends, family, strangers, love, faith, prayers and the Lord walking threw this with us it would have been a much harder path to travel. It's changed our lives, but also blessed us.

Sincerely,

Ernie & Cindy Long

"Everything can be taken from man except the last of human freedom, his ability to choose his own attitude in any given set of circumstances - to choose his own way."

– Victor Frankl

...his favorite game is playing cards and he enjoys camping. When he grows up he would like to be a doctor.

Ethan Long

Ethan was airlifted from Kalispell, Montana to Seattle Children's Hospital when he was a day old. He had been born with an undeveloped aortic valve and fortunately; the doctor recognized the problem immediately. His first surgery was performed when Ethan was a week old. More surgery was planned for him at age 3, but at 18 months, his health didn't pass muster. Doctors implanted a mechanical heart valve instead.

In his letter, Ethan describes his latest operation. He is doing well. He has a stuffed rabbit named Freddy and would one day like to teach a monkey to ride a skateboard. Ethan has lots of energy. In fact, his dad says that if a pacemaker gives you that much energy, he'd like to have one, too!

Ethan Long

Dear Andy,

    My name is Ethan. I remember a big operation on my heart I had last year. They took out my artificial aortic valve and put my pulmonary valve in were my aortic valve was, they then gave me a different persons valve. I was very scared and very mad. My mom got to go in the operating room with me till I went to sleep, but I still cried. I didn't know if I was going to die. It hurts when you come out of surgery too. I got really mad when I woke up because I wanted some water really bad and they said I couldn't have any. I didn't know why I couldn't . Then they didn't have a T.V. there so I couldn't watch cartoons so that made me mad also. They put a tube down my throat, I didn't like that, it makes your throat sore. They stuck one in my neck too, that hurt really bad. They stuck needles in my arms for stuff to go into me to help make me better, but it doesn't seem like it when it hurts. After a while they moved me so I had a T.V. and they let me have just a little water. I always wanted more but they said no. I got really mad when they tried to get me up to go to the bathroom that hurt so bad I screamed, yelled, and cried. I was glad when they put me back in bed and told them they better not do that again. My back hurt so bad all the time. That is what hurt the worst. My mom would rub it and rub it and it still hurt. Then they said I should eat some things but I couldn't eat. After awhile they made me eat two bites of some things or they said I couldn't go upstairs to a different room. So I did and then when they moved me up there, it made me throw up. But the next day I woke up hungry so I ate and then I started feeling better. Mom said I smiled for the first time and that her boy was back. I was sure glad when I got to get out of the hospital to go to my grandma's and grandpa's.

    It's not fun to have operations but they make you better, so if you have one you have to try to remember that, you talk to Jesus too. I use to not be able to do a lot of sports and running before, they did this operation and now I can, that made me happy. I don't have to take the medicine that made me bleed real bad if I got hurt, so that I really like too. You just have to do some of the things you really don't want to, and let them do things to you that hurt but they do them to make you better, so you have to do them even if you don't like it.

    I want to say hi to the people at Children's Miracle Network. I made it through my really big operation. Thank you for letting me go to Disney World, that was the best thing that I got to do, it was so fun, everyone was so nice to me. I miss you all.

Thank you,

Ethan Long

FUTURE ARTIST

...would like to be on the Seattle Super Sonics Basketball team and play center. His favorite holiday is fourth of July because of the fireworks.

Jon Matthew Penprase

Matt is a student at Parkview High School in Springfield, Missouri. As you will read in his letter, Matt isn't allowed to participate in contact sports anymore, but he has become extremely proficient on the golf course and archery range. He collects coins and sports cards and works as a board engineer for KLFG, a local radio station that broadcasts baseball games.

Matt wants to be an architect when he finishes college, and just between you and me, he already has made a name for himself in that area of expertise. He has had his artwork displayed outside his state representative's office and at a local art museum. Matt is a champion in many areas of his life.

Jon Matthew Penprase
3116 W. Broadmoor St.
Springfield, MO 65807

Andy Andrews
P. O. Box 2761
Gulf Shores, AL 36547

Dear Andy:

In September of 1995, I had a brain abscess, resulting in four craniotomies. I was in a coma and was paralyzed on one side of my body for about 10 days. I was in the hospital for more than a month, and I missed almost a whole semester of school. After it was all over with, I learned that I'd been given only a 10 percent chance of surviving.

One thing I learned is that you can get very seriously ill in a very short time and for no obvious reason. Even if you're being careful, you never know what might happen. On a more personal level, I learned how important I am to my family. Relatives came to the hospital frequently to check on me and my progress.

Being as critically ill as I was, I think I appreciate things more now. I wish I could play basketball, but my surgeon has permanently prohibited me from playing contact sports. As much as I would like to play, I know it is much more important that I lived through what happened.

I would like to thank Children's Miracle Network for their support for me and my family, but especially for providing the ventilator that kept me alive when I was not strong enough to breathe on my own. They also provided the heart monitor that was used for me in the Pediatric Intensive Care Unit.

Anyone facing a serious illness or a tough recovery from one has to work hard to get better. It isn't easy, and it isn't any fun, but if you want it bad enough, you can do it.

Sincerely,

Matt Penprase

Matt Penprase

Dustin, Kim, Skylar, Martin and Josh

AMAZING DOCTORS

They love what they do, but it will never compare to the love and devotion they have for their children. This family is unstoppable and it seems that Josh, Dustin and Skylar are at the head of the line.

Drs. Martin and Kim Frey

This is a very unusual letter in that it was written by parents who both happen to be doctors. That fact makes this letter all the more amazing.

Kim attended Barnard College as an undergraduate and went on to earn her M.D. at New York University School of Medicine in 1982. She did her residency in general surgery Montefiore Hospital and the Albert Einstein College of Medicine finishing in 1987. For two years, Kim taught residents and medical students at Downstate as Assistant Professor of Surgery.

Marty attended Washington University in St. Louis. After four years of graduate research, he received his Masters Degree in Pulmonary Physiology from the University of California in San Francisco. Marty received his M.D. from the George Washington School of Medicine and immediately joined a residency program at Montefiore Hospital where he met Kim.

Marty and Kim married in 1987 and almost two years later moved to Sarasota, Florida where they live today. Both are as successful in their family lives as they are professionally. They now have three boys — Josh, Dustin, and Skylar.

Drs. Martin and Kim Frey

Andy Andrews
P. O. Box 2761
Gulf Shores, AL 36547

Dear Andy,

When my husband and I think of all that has happened since Joshua was born, it is hard to think of it, and of course him, as anything other than a blessing. If someone gave me a magic wand and I could heal my son, naturally I would, but I would do so starting from now, not from when he was born, because I am so grateful for all the wisdom, strength and growth that sometimes comes only from pain and struggle. We are different people, and different physicians, with so much more gratitude for all of our countless blessings. Our whole family, including our other two sons, is different, and of course Joshua is an amazing spirit who touches lives wherever he goes.

We waited until we were done with our medical training to have any children and so we were thrilled when Josh was born in 1989. Other than something the doctor called "neurological immaturity" which was never really explained, no one seemed to notice any problem with him at first. He was very intense, startled very easily and often, and didn't sleep much. He was unhappy and screaming a lot of the time, despite everything we could think of to quiet him. All of his motor milestones were very late, and despite our concerns, the pediatrician kept calling it a "normal variant". He accused us of being overly concerned physician parents, but finally around 15 months, we insisted that he see a pediatric neurologist. This doctor agreed that it was within a normal range, but suggested he be reevaluated, although we were never given this bit of information. At the age of two, he still could not walk, except holding onto both my hands and then still very unsteadily. He did not transfer an object hand to hand, but would put it down and then pick it up with the other hand, it was extremely difficult for him to use both hands at the same time. He was obviously very bright and his language development was normal to accelerated.

At the age of 21/2, despite objections from our pediatrician, we started him in physical and occupational therapy. The therapists seemed to agree with us that there was something wrong, and diagnosed him with "tactile defensiveness". This was what our pediatrician considered a vague catchall term, which he did not acknowledge, and because he did not carry a physician's diagnosis, his therapy was not covered and we had to pay for it out of pocket. We felt frustrated and alone at this juncture, and after a year of therapy, not knowing if it was helping or if the improvements we were seeing would have been part of his normal development anyway, we switched pediatricians, to get yet another opinion, and hopefully some guidance.

The second pediatrician was much more responsive and immediately recognized that Joshua was not moving and developing normally. He sent us for an evaluation with the pediatric neurologists and developmental specialists at the Johns Hopkins University School of Medicine. They also were impressed that something was wrong and after several days of testing were pretty sure that it was a neuropathy (catchall term for abnormality of the nerves). They needed one last test to be sure and that was a nerve conduction study, and then if this were positive, they would schedule him for nerve and muscle biopsies. At this juncture, we were scared because some of the possibilities carried with them the risk of worsening of the condition and possible death. I guess this had always been in the back of Marty's mind and of course being physicians we did know too much in some ways and had already done a lot of reading, and imagining the worst-case scenarios. For my part, whether it was a mother's intuition, or just self-protection through denial, I always knew in my heart that Joshua would be okay.

The people we met at Johns Hopkins were wonderful and treated us with the utmost compassion, unfortunately though they couldn't do the test there for another week, so we went home to have them done at a children's hospital nearby. Being physicians we checked it out and requested the head of the department, which turned out to be a big mistake.

Joshua by now was 3&1/2, and was able to walk, albeit clumsily and with a lot of falls, and he could even run. He had to shift from foot to foot for balance and walk and stand with his feet pretty far apart to give him a broader base of support, because be couldn't feel his feet or tell where he was in space without that constant input of vibration coming up from them. He also was very sensitive to tastes and textures and had a very strong gag response and vomited frequently. He needed to be sedated for the procedure with an oral liquid medicine. This alone took over an hour and involved forcing it into him and having it vomited back in our faces several times. He was miserable and so were we, not to mention, anxious and annoyed that the doctor had never even examined him prior to his sedation. Finally he was asleep and the doctor came in. No introduction or pleasantries, he merely informed us that we could stay in the room if we did not utter a sound. He then proceeded to perform the tests, by sticking needles into his arms and legs at various points and measuring the muscle responses and the time for an impulse to travel from one point to another. When he was finished, he turned around to us, and the only words he said were, "this is severe and it is progressive, it's a good thing the diaphragm is so well innervated," then he walked out of the room.

We have never in all our medical training or practice seen such an unbelievable lack of compassion or bedside manner, and to add to it he was carelessly giving erroneous information because he had never seen Joshua awake and had no idea that he was already performing at a level that the tests he had just performed said were impossible. At this point Marty fell to his knees, but I did not believe this for a minute and confronted him in his office and insisted that he call the people at Johns Hopkins immediately and discuss it with them. They of course (having seen Josh awake and having other test data), said that he couldn't draw those conclusions from the limited data he had, and reassured us immeasurably. We tell this part of the story in detail, because if 2 doctors can get treated like this, we can only imagine how some other people get treated and you must never accept a doctor's word unless you are sure he has all the facts, which include your observations and intuitions. We do not say this to discredit doctors in any way, but they are after all human, and ultimately, one of the most important lessons we continue to learn in this journey is that we have to trust ourselves. We wanted to find an expert to tell us what to do and what was happening, but fate continually conspired to make us step up. It turned out that after all the tests, including the nerve and muscle biopsies, Joshua's condition did not fit into any known category of disease. In other words after all this they still did not know what was wrong with him and if it would get worse or not. For any parents this would be extremely difficult, but for 2 doctors it was agony.

It was especially hard for Marty, who couldn't stop imagining the worst. He saw Joshua in a wheelchair, then on a respirator, and finally dead at a young age. He lost 11 pounds over the 2 weeks after the tests were done, and would often break down in tears. It was a strain on our marriage, because I was inherently optimistic and felt that although I believed Joshua would be fine, if he wasn't, I wanted to make the best of the time he did have, and I didn't want him to pick up on Marty's fears and sadness. I also would have liked more support and room for my own fears. However, it turned out that quite possibly the very thing that threatened our marriage saved it.

Marty had always been extremely concrete and scientific and refused to realize how much choice you had in how you experienced your life, but because of the severe pain he experienced, what with the helplessness and lack of control over what would happen with Josh, he started to open up and look at other paradigms. Because of what he has learned, he has become an even better husband and father and a mentor and coach to many of his employees and friends. He is now optimistic and looking for the good in every situation. He now asks himself when faced with a challenge, "What could be great about this?".

We learned in the ensuing years, that we had to be Joshua's advocates, and that experts or not, no one knew him as well or had observed him as keenly as we had. They couldn't always tell us what he could and couldn't do, so that sometimes we had to learn by trial and error what we could expect of him. The challenge was to allow him, and even to push him to do as much as he could for himself so that he would be independent but of course to be there to nurture and support him when he couldn't do something and make sure he didn't get too frustrated to the point of discouragement. No small task as the parents of any child will tell you, let alone a differently abled child. In many ways the challenge has gotten bigger as he has gotten older and become aware of his differences. He sometimes tries to manipulate us and act helpless, and at other times wants to do things that are clearly beyond his capabilities. All in all though we have found that he knows himself and what he can and cannot do and we let him try most things he wants to.

We try very hard not to overprotect him or to impose limits on him. After all, the tests the local doctor did that day say he can't walk or run, but he does. He also plays basketball and baseball and swims and rides a special 3-wheel bike. We even let him try Tae Kwon Do and he got to a purple belt, but because of his foot drop (it is hard for him to lift the toe or front of his foot up due to muscle weakness) he badly stubbed his toe too many times and we were worried he would do damage.

Some of the hardest things to deal with now that he is older are his own doubts and fears and feelings of being different. The questions he asks, like "Why did God make me different? Why couldn't he make everybody normal? " These are tough questions, but we believe and tell Josh that there is a purpose for everything and everyone, and many lessons to be learned from challenges. We tell him that everyone has a disability, but some show more that others and everyone has special and unique qualities and he certainly has those.

When I first got pregnant and had Josh, I was struck by a new sense of vulnerability. It seemed inconceivably painful to imagine anything happening to this precious baby of mine. One of the most important things I think we both have learned is that when you have to step up and handle things, you do, and you find you are possessed of resources you never imagined you had. You can also learn that things you once thought would be your worst nightmare can turn out to be a blessing if you look for the blessing in them. It is always there.

We have been privileged to meet many other families with challenged children in our journey. Mostly we feel that we are blessed compared with what so many of these families have to deal with, but as we have gotten to know them and their children, we have realized that there is a blessing and an inspiration in each of their stories. I have watched the indomitable spirit of these children, most closely with my son, and watched how they have inspired people. They are truly heroes. Most of them put up with more frustration in a day than many of us deal within a lifetime.

The other thing that strikes you as you get to know them is that like the blind person who has incredible hearing or smell, when God takes away something, he gives back something else. Joshua has the most uncanny charisma and charm. People fall in love with him wherever he goes, and he is the most loving and outgoing child, amazingly unselfconscious about his clumsiness and falling. Much more so than most normal children I know, including his brothers. Once he came running into the kitchen playing a superhero yelling "Mom I'm strong", and then proceeded to fall flat on his face, at which point he looked at me sheepishly and added "and clumsy", and we both broke up laughing. Another time, when I was pregnant with our youngest son, Skylar, Joshua stubbed his toe very badly, and asked me very angrily why did he have these nerves and his brother Dustin (our middle son) didn't. Then after I answered him as best I could, he looked at me and said, "I hope the baby doesn't have these nerves". I started to cry, he was only 6, and I had no idea he could even understand that concept let alone have that much compassion. I told him that the baby was very lucky to have a big brother like him, who was so loving and would protect him and help him.

All in all, life with Joshua has brought richness and a joy that I wouldn't trade for anything. We have grown immeasurably as people, as a couple, as parents, and as doctors. We have learned to enjoy the "precious present" as Dr. Spencer Johnson calls it in his book of the same name. We have learned immense gratitude and not to take things for granted, but to appreciate them and to express that appreciation to God and the people we love, every day. Most of all, we have learned what I believe to be the ultimate lesson in everything this life sends your way, and that is that it is up to you. It is up to you to step up and take responsibility, to trust your inner knowing. We are so much more powerful than we have any idea. It is up to you to choose the attitude with which you will face the challenges that are an integral part of life. Whether you will resent them and resist them, or be open to the lessons and the blessings they have to offer you. It is up to you whether you will waste the time you have worrying about things that may never happen, or enjoying the many blessings right in front of you.

Thank you for the opportunity to tell our story Andy. We hope that it can help or inspire someone who is just starting out on the journey with a disabled child or as a disabled child, that there are lessons and blessings in every situation if you look for them.

Warmly,

Drs. Martin & Kim Frey

FUTURE TEACHER

...his favorite song is Iris by the Goo Goo Dolls. His favorite musical instrument is the drums and has been playing them for over 5 years. He likes Bugs Bunny because of his sly ways.

Bradley Lewon

To have one's life changed by an accident is a hard thing for a person to understand. A child must find such a situation infinitely harder. Bradley, however, has a firm grasp on the reality of such an occurrence. The last line of his letter states: "You are still the same person." Bradley has been able to use the misfortune of several years ago to comfort and inspire others who have faced a similar challenge.

Bradley lives in a loving home with his mother, father, sister, and brother. He loves to hunt and fish and expects to be a math teacher as an adult because he enjoys solving problems and helping people.

BRADLEY LEWON

Andy Andrews
PO Box 3709
Gulf Shores, AL 36547

Dear Andy,

On April 27, 1991, my brother and I headed out to the garage in the backyard with a lighter I had found in the house. It was about 12:30 p.m. and at 1:00, I was planning on meeting a bunch of friends at the ball field to play some baseball. What I didn't know was that what was about to happen was going to change my plans that day and for the rest of my life. My brother, Kevin, and I were lighting some old dead leaves and sticks that were in the garage. I saw an old gas can in the corner and decided to use some of that to make things neater. I poured some gas on a stick and lit it on fire. After that burned for a bit, I thought I would pour some gas on top of the flame. Bad idea. As I did this the flames flared up. Kevin and I both fell back from the flames. I dropped the gas can and when I turned around to see what happened, I saw the gas can sitting upright with a little flame just sitting there on the end of the nozzle. Being only 10 years old and not knowing the real danger in mixing gas and fire, I decided to run and grab the gas can before anything happened. As my hands were only inches away, the gas can exploded.

The flames covered my body from my waist up on my front side. The first thing I did was "stop, drop, and roll." After I did this for awhile, I ran outside the garage and started rolling around on the ground. By this time, my brother had ran inside and told my dad who then called the ambulance. He came running outside and put what little bit that was still burning on me out with his hands. The ambulance took me part of the way to the hospital where a life flight helicopter picked me up and took me the rest of the way.

43 1/2% of my body had third degree burns. The doctor gave me only a 50% chance of living. I spent 73 days in the hospital the first time I was in and went back many times for more reconstructive surgeries. Throughout this ordeal, I have had a lot of painful physical therapy and over 35 surgeries with some set backs during that time. The doctors were amazed that I didn't have any eye damage because they stated my eyes had to be open during the explosion since my eyelids were not burned. Also, I didn't have any lung damage even though I inhaled a lot of heat and smoke. These "miracles" along with just being alive were God's answers to the many people that were praying for me. Throughout the days, as everyone continued to pray, God continued to heal me.

While in the hospital, I got to know all the nurses and doctors very well. They became like a second family to me. With the help and support of them along with my family and friends, I was able to recover much more easily from this tragedy.

I also got to be a part of the Children's Miracle Network while I was in the hospital and have continued to do so for 8 years. The Children's Miracle Network has made it possible for me and several other children who have been burned to go to a burn camp where we are able to meet others who have been through the same thing. It allows us to make new friends and just have a good time. I would like to take this chance to say THANKS to the people with the Children's Miracle Network for doing all they have done for the children and the hospitals in the region.

P.O. BOX 165 • RANDOLPH, NE 68771

I've learned through all of this ordeal to not give up and to take it one day at a time. Also, even if you have scars from burns or some other illness, you are still the same person inside so always be yourself. Don't worry about what others might think or say because <u>you are still the same person!!!</u>

Sincerely,

Bradley Lewon

The pessimist finds fault;

The optimist discovers a remedy.

The pessimist seeks sympathy;

The optimist spreads cheer.

The pessimist criticizes circumstances;

The optimist changes conditions.

The pessimist complains about the apple seeds;

The optimist plants them.

The pessimist imagines impending peril;

The optimist sees signs of prosperity.

The pessimist disparages;

The optimist encourages.

The pessimist creates loneliness;

The optimist finds friends.

The pessimist nibbles at the negative;

The optimist is nourished by the positive.

The pessimist builds barriers;

The optimist removes roadblocks.

The pessimist invents trouble;

The optimist enriches the environment.

– Will Ward

HIGH ACADEMIC ACHIEVER

...he is 10 years old and has a terrific life. He loves bugs, animals and nature. When he grows up he wants to be a scientist to find cures for diseases.

Shayn Lansden

Shayn, born four weeks early due to a hole in the amniotic sack, began life rather suddenly. By the age of five weeks, surgery was necessary to save this tender young life. He was diagnosed with Pyloric Stenosis; a disorder in which food in the stomach is not able to pass through to the intestine, but rather is vomited out depriving the body of the nourishment it needs.

After surgery, Shayn seemed as normal as any other infant, but by the age of one, he was in and out of the emergency room more than four times a week. Throughout the following year, Shayn's parents were desperately seeking answers to this unyielding illness without success. Finally, he was diagnosed with asthma and with a name attached to his ailment, Shayn's parents felt a sense of relief.

Shayn's asthma has now been controlled, thus his quality of life has increased tremendously. Shayn swims, plays football, and receives top honors in school for academics.

Mr. Andy Andrews
PO Box 3709
Gulf Shores, Alabama 36547

Dear Andy,

I have just celebrated my 10th birthday! This is a big deal for me because I am thankful for each and every day I am alive. I have almost lost my life three times and have had many other close calls. I always thought I was normal, whatever that may be, yet I have found that things most people take for granted, I give thanks for the opportunity to experience; like playing in fluffy white snow in the middle of winter or splashing in a puddle left from a soft spring rain or even feeling the warmth of the sun on my face while riding my bike to the park. These precious gifts of life, as simple as they may seem, are very special to me.

I was born with asthma, although I was not diagnosed with it until the age of 2 1/2. It was when I had pneumonia that a wonderful woman, Dr. Pincus, discovered that all of the hospital visits and treatments I had endured over the past year were due to asthma. During my stay at National Jewish Medical and Research Center, I was treated for the pneumonia, as well as my asthma. I progressively worsened and the doctors, nurses and my parents did everything within their power to help save my life. I almost did not make it, but with all the love and determination from the medical staff and my parents, along with a lot of prayers, I pulled through and was granted this miracle of life.

At that time I did not realize how different I was from other kids. All of the trips to the hospital, the daily medicines and the restrictions I had, somehow seemed normal to me. I knew no different. While other kids were outside playing and having fun, I would usually be in the hospital struggling for each breath ....and my life.

Medicines are part of my daily routine. I also have to be monitored daily with a peak flow meter to make sure I am within reasonable limits. Because of all this I attend a school on the campus of the hospital where nurses help care for me. I travel 60 miles per day to attend this school in order to insure my health and quality of life. For me, there is no alternative. There are many things I am still not able to do because of my asthma; like playing soccer, being around animals and going to the circus or even going to eat in some restaurants because of the smoke. Because my immune system has been compromised, I also cannot be around many of my friends when they are sick and sometimes that includes not going to birthday parties. At times, I feel very alone... very different. Due to all of these differences in my life, I have learned to care about others and respect their feelings.

I have also learned in my short lifetime the fragility of life and importance of living it to the fullest. You never know when your time here may end and always giving your best is very important. Over the past three years, I have experienced three of my classmates passing on. It definitely allowed me the opportunity to reflect on life's importance. The sadness and sorrow that comes with it is painful and not easily forgotten and is therefore the forefront to pushing on and always being thankful for each breath I take.

Fortunately, I have a great deal of support from my parents and a few people at school. The very special people at school are Haley Tepe, Mary Morrissey, Jim Gianvito, Michelle Freas and Barbara O'Regan. Without these people my life would not be as wonderful as it is. Each giving, caring and loving in their own special way has helped me to be a better person. They have each set such a superb example of love and excellence in life for me that I know I can do anything I set my mind and heart to. I am very thankful to each of them, as I have been able to achieve many goals and dreams.

Children's Miracle Network has also been a tremendous influence in my life. So many special people, like Barbara O'Regan, who have offered me an opportunity to excel and succeed in life. I am very grateful and I thank each and every soul involved with and contributing to Children's Miracle Network with every breath I take for the love and support they have given me. If not for the hard work and heartwarming generosity they continuously share with myself and others, life would not be so rich.

My hope for you is to take one day at a time and through the trials of life, no matter what they are----always give it your best and always, always believe..............in *yourself*........and ....in *miracles*!

Sincerely,

Shayn Lansden

Shayn Lansden

He spends his free time volunteering at the Siouxland Regional Cancer Center and is very active in his church youth group.

Austin Rodriguez

In May 1997, thirteen year old Austin went to St. Lukes emergency room after suffering a series of severe headaches and nausea. A CT scan confirmed a tumor deep inside his brain. Thus began a regimen of surgeries, radiation, and chemotherapy that consumed Austin's life for the next several months. Throughout his unbelievable ordeal, Austin called upon his faith in God to comfort him and his parents. His doctors were impressed with Austin's personality and his great attitude during this time of misfortune and suffering.

Austin is a fan of Iowa Hawkeye's basketball and would love to one day travel to Europe in order to search for the Arc of the Covenant. He plays the alto saxophone and intends to become a coordinator for Children's Miracle Network in order to help children like himself.

Austin Rodriguez

Dear Andy,

The biggest challenge in my life was in the year of 1997. On May 4th I found out I had a tumor in my brain. At first I cried, but then a lady who goes to my church told me God would heal me. Those words dried up my tears. The next day I had my surgery. A few days later Dr. Ragnarsson told my parents that the tumor was malignant. Later that month I started chemo at Children's Hospital in Omaha, Nebraska. I became very sick from the chemo drugs. After each treatment the medicine would kill my blood cells, forcing me to be in the hospital getting blood transfusions. But through it all I said "God will heal me".

The time between treatments was so long that another tumor grew. After I heard the news, I said "This is just a setback, God will heal me!". After Dr. Ragnarsson removed the second tumor I started six weeks of radiation. The radiation scared me because I would close my eyes during the treatments and see a blue light and smell a weird smell. I received radiation to my brain and spinal cord, but through it all I kept a positive attitude.

I had an MRI on Jan. 13, 1998 and got the results back on Jan. 15. It was negative! The second I heard that, I danced around the Cancer Center. I said God would heal me and he did!

One positive experience that came out of my sickness was that I was honored by being chosen to represent Iowa at the CMN Champions Across America telethon. They treated us like royalty and I got to meet the rest of the Miracle Children from across the US and Canada. It was a great experience and I am proud to be a part of such a wonderful organization.

My experience that year helped me realize you need to live life to the fullest and to never take it for granted. I have been cancer free for one year now and I praise God every day for my health. I'm back in school and each day I get stronger and look forward to living a normal life again.

Thank-you for letting me share with you the most important year of my life.

Sincerely,

Austin
Rodriguez

BLACK BELT IN KARATE

...if he had three wishes he would wish for good health, happiness and good friends and family. This would make him the happiest boy on earth. He would also like to travel back in time and help Dr. King in the fight against racial discrimination.

David Farmer

"The goal to remain upbeat is important to me because your outward behavior both reflects on you and affects many other people." This sentence from David's letter was a powerful testimony to me. After reading what he has been through, this attitude is as incredible as it is inspirational.

David loves to cook and eat. Lemon meringue pie and crepes are among his favorites. He collects spoons and bells and enjoys water skiing and roller blading with his family. David's favorite baseball team is Atlanta and one day he'd like to play third base or pitch for the Braves.

David Farmer

Dear Andy ,

My name is David Farmer. In the summer of 1996, I was diagnosed with ALL (Acute Lymphocytic Leukemia). It started as excrutiating pains in my joints. We went to our pediatrician, and she couldn't diagnose what was wrong. I finally had a bone marrow aspiration. As soon as the marrow was removed, the doctor knew immediately that it was cancer.

I was immediately sent me to the Egleston Children's Hospital at Emory University and chemotherapy was initiated. Fortunately, I soon got better and they sent me home for regular outpatient chemo. Soon I started having really bad headaches. We went to the doctor and they did a CT scan. We were told that I had accumulated brain lesions due to one of the chemo drugs called L-asparaginase. As a result, I had to learn to walk, talk, and take care of myself. Soon another problem occurred - severe abdominal pains which doctors eventually diagnosed as infectious pancreatitis. The surgeons had to do a partial pancreatectomy, and I wasn't able to eat anything by mouth for many months thereafter.

The battle wasn't over yet, we had to find a matching bone marrow donor or I wasn't going to live. We searched all across America and Europe, but failed. Finally we went to a Christmas party held by Camp Sunshine, a camp for pediatric cancer patients. When we went inside, Tara Taneski, the bone marrow coordinator at Egleston, was walking toward us with a smile from ear to ear. We exchanged greetings and no later had we done that than Tara exclaimed, "We found a 5 out of 6 match from a donor from South Korea!" South Korea was my birth home. That moment was probably the happiest moment for my entire family, but especially for my parents. During the rest of the party, they seemed to walk on air because I had received another chance at life.

In February of 1997, the bone marrow was flown from South Korea and then transplanted into me. The next few months I developed graft versus host disease (GVHD), a potentially lethal condition in which my new immune system damaged cells lining the digestive tract. Later because of a temporary decline in the function of my new immune system, I also developed a severe systemic infection producing additional brain lesions and seizures. I was comatose in the Egleston pediatric ICU and nearly died. Once again, I underwent extensive rehabilitation to regain function and be able to perform normal every-day activities.

Recently I have had to deal with a type of anorexia in which I am hungry and eating, but not gaining weight. This complication resulted from the many leukemia treatments. I also have a bone disease (avascular necrosis) due to the previous chronic use of steroids, and now require a wheelchair to get around, although I can walk short distances. Just recently, I have also developed an airway obstruction near my vocal chords that has required the use of a tracheostomy (a tube inserted into my windpipe).

Throughout these many hardships, I have attempted to maintain a cheery disposition and attitude although on the inside I was fighting a battle with depression stemming from chronic health problems and brain lesions. It has not always been easy to remain upbeat, but this goal is important to me because your outward behavior both reflects on you and affects many other people.

All throughout these ordeals I was able to keep my sanity by maintaining faith in God, keeping a good attitude, and talking to others about what I was feeling. If you don't talk to people about what's wrong or where you're hurting, they can't help you. Another thing that kept me going was the many volunteers that would come and play with the patients, read to us, hold bingo games Thursday nights, or just sit next to us and keep us company. A lot of support from other people inspired me to keep fighting too. Support from my family, friends, doctors, nurses, hospital staff, friends at Camp Sunshine, Leukemia Society Team-in-Training participants like Peter Nicolatis, and even celebrities. My family refers to the staff at the Egleston Hospital as "angels".

These many setbacks have affected my feelings and how I view the world. I try to think of good things that will come in life, and I guess that this is some advice that others going through tough times might find beneficial. Also, it is important to keep in mind what is important in your life. In my case, what's important is having faith in God, being with my family and my friends, going places and meeting people, and basically living life to it's fullest. Take care and God bless.

Sincerely,

David Farmer

David Farmer

"I know God will not give me anything I can't handle. I just wish He didn't trust me so much."

– Mother Teresa

Andrea, Mickey and Evita

FIGHTING CHAMPION MOTHER

...full time mother and wife. Continuously giving in-home therapy to her daughter. Gets in return 100% love and care from her family.

Evita Valero

Evita and Teddy, parents of sweet little Andrea, were born in the Philippines. Evita was a flight attendant for a major airline when her child was born while Teddy worked as the owner of his own business. After living out of a suitcase for several years, Evita retired to be a full time mother.

Because of the love and care they were shown during Andreas' miraculous recovery, Evita and Teddy have become actively involved with the Children's Miracle Network. Evita also works as a primary teacher at their church in Pasadena, California. Andreas continues to improve and the whole family continues to give of themselves to others.

Evita Valero

Andy Andrews
P. O. Box 2761
Gulf Shores, AL 36561

Dear Andy,

Thank you for paving the way for us to reach out and share our trial and triumphs in life. It's a way for us to let other people know that during the saddest and hardest times of life you will never be alone, and to witness that *miracles happen - one at a time*.

It was 1992, when everything was coming up roses. We had our first and only daughter, Andrea. She loves to dance, sing, and swim. At the age of three she learned to speak 4 languages: English, Chinese, Malay, and tag along. Teddy, my husband, was a Hotellier and has worked in and out of the country in prestigious hotels. I was a flight attendant for a major airline. I then decided to leave my job and enjoy motherhood. Teddy was assigned a job at a resort-hotel in Malaysia and we decided to tag along. Andrea was only a year old at this time.

When Teddy decided to retire and venture into his own business, our luck started to change. Things went well for a short time, then our business suffered a major setback. A setback that took our life's savings and took it's toll on us as a family. We ended up rooming in with some friends. Being in a foreign land without friends and family is quite possibly the most devastating feeling we've ever had. It was actually Andrea who encouraged us to go back to America and start over again. At the tender age of three, without being bitter towards our situation, she had better judgment than Teddy and I. Andrea constantly told us, not to worry, things will be better soon. So in June of 1995, we headed back to America with only a few dollars in our pocket.

We enjoyed being back in the states and so did Andrea. However, the happiness was short lived, for after a year without any warning, Andrea became ill. She was suffering from a life threatening illness called AVM or simply a brain aneurysm. This almost took her life. With no money, and no jobs, how could we handle this. I was so devastated, I was numb, I didn't know what to think or feel. But I can tell you this, God has His own way of helping each of us.

At this particular time, we were living in Los Angeles where Children's Hospital of Los Angeles happens to be. This is our first sign of a miracle. Andrea was admitted, and no time was wasted. Her brain stem was bleeding, and she was in very critical condition. Right away, I put my daughter's life into the hands of chief nuero surgeon, Dr. Gordon McComb (this is our second miracle). An eleven-hour surgery followed, during which the doctors eliminated, re-sectioned, and cauterized the remaining arterial venous malformation. My daughter's life was miraculously saved.

After surgery, however, Andrea remained in a vegetative state having totally lost all of her motor skills. There is a long journey on the road to recovery. No promises were made on how long recovery would take or how much Andrea would recover. I refused to believe that she would live the rest of her life in a vegetative state. I prayed and prayed, and left everything in the hands of God.

Soon we were transferred to the rehab unit at Children's Hospital of Los Angeles where we stayed for four months. During our stay Andrea worked hard at physical therapy, occupational therapy, and speech therapy. Everyday, twice a day, Andrea worked hard to build her body back up. She went from a vegetative state to being able to chew, swallow and lift her head. Then she went to a wheel chair, a walker, and finally walking.

…Continued

Andrea's therapy completely turned my priorities in life around. My plans to have a big house and send my daughter to the best school in town had to take the back seat. Now my priorities are simple pleasures, lots of love, and appreciation of life, and thanking God for each day that we are together and alive.

Sincerely,

Evita Valero

MIRACLES OF LOVE

I WAS SICK AND I WAS SAD,
IT WAS BRAIN ANUERYSM THAT I HAD.
YOU AND I FOUGHT FOR MY LIFE,
WHEN I HAD TO GO UNDER THE KNIFE.

NOW IT'S OVER AND DONE,
ALL THOSE TANGLED VEINS WERE GONE.
ANOTHER LIFE I HAVE TO FACE,
THINGS LIKE THESE IS JUST A FATE,

THERE'S NO SUCH THING AS TOO LATE,
I KNOW I CAN COME UP WITH AN ACE.
IT'S NOT EASY FOR ME TO PULL THROUGH,
BUT I MADE IT TOO! BECAUSE OF YOU.

YOU GAVE ME ANOTHER CHANCE,
SO LET ME SHOW YOU THAT I CAN DANCE!
JUST ONE OF YOUR MIRACLES THAT I BECOME A STAR,
YOUR LOVE AND CARE MADE ME COME THIS FAR.

FOR THIS, LET ME SAY OH PLEASE!
THANKS A MILLION FOR MAKING ME A ....CHAMPION !!!

BY : ANDREA V. EDORIA

CHAMPION SKIIER

...would like to bungy jump and be on the National Ski Team. When he gets older he would like to be a journalist or a master communicator.

Josh Sundquist

I am looking forward to shaking hands with Josh one day. This is an amazing guy. When he was nine years old, he was diagnosed with a rare form of bone cancer in his left leg called Ewing's Sarcoma. Josh was given a fifty/fifty chance to live. After three chemotherapy treatments proved ineffective at shrinking the tumor, his leg was amputated at the hip.

Rather than feeling sorry for himself, Josh started his life anew facing challenges with a steely eye and a terrific sense of humor. Josh is an Eagle Scout so it will come as no surprise that he also has won several skiing races. Josh mountain bikes, swims, and is currently a member of the varsity wrestling team at his high school.

 Josh Sundquist

Hey Andy!

I usually laugh when I see pictures of me when I was eight years old. I kept my hair so perfect! Every day I would carefully comb it, adding in more and more hair gel until I was satisfied that every hair was in its exact position.

Then I remember when I was nine years old, sitting in the UVA children's medical center terrace after my surgery, talking to my parents. We were talking about chemotherapy, and then they told me about my hair. I started crying as soon as they told me it would fall out. Besides that, I would be bald for the entire year that I was on treatment!

I never realized how important it was for me to keep my hair in place! I was just devastated. But God was planning a way to cheer me up. While lying in my hospital room, I got a phone call. It was my little brother's friend, Ryan. He told me that he was going to shave his head so I wouldn't feel as alone!

Then his mom came up with an idea. Why not invite other friends to shave their heads, too?

The idea caught on, and some moms thought it would be easier if everyone got their heads shaved in my backyard! A date was set, and there was an announcement in our church bulletin. Then the newspaper found out about the event, and a reporter came to my house for an interview the night before.

When the day came, eighteen boys came to my house to get their heads shaved! While a couple of moms performed the "chemo cuts" in the back yard, skinhead boys ate food and played soccer. It was a party! The next day, huge color pictures and an article titled "On the Cutting Edge of Friendship" spoke of the love of my friends.

Some of the boys were younger than me, others were older, and there was even one father! My dad offered to shave his head also, but I suggested that it might not grow back. Hey-I was only nine.

Sometimes I think about that pale, bald little boy who spent weeks lying in a hospital bed. So young, yet filled with that relentless determination to live. I have learned to live with this kind of courage. When I was bald, I looked to a day when I would have hair. Now, when I have hair, I look day by day to building my life around goals.

Josh

Linda and Paul

THEIR FAITH IN GOD SUSTAINS THEM

...their faith in God has given them the courage to face anything that is sent their way. Their family has endured many hardships, but the lessons they learned made them stronger and wiser.

Paul and Linda Sundquist

Paul was born in Minneapolis, but moved to the Washington, DC area when he was five. Linda is from Norfolk, Virginia and met Paul at the College of William and Mary in Williamsburg. They were married a year after their college graduation. Paul is an accounting manager for a metal company and Linda home schools their four children.

Paul and Linda needed the lessons they learned during Josh's chemotherapy again this past year. In November, Linda was diagnosed with Lymphoma and underwent chemo for five months. In the midst of another difficult situation, their faith in God sustained them and their friends and church family supported them. Linda is now in remission and they are praying for another miraculous healing from cancer.

Paul and Linda Sundquist

Dear Andy,

When we first learned that our son, Joshua, had bone cancer at nine years old, we were devastated. Once we discovered that the treatment was a year of chemotherapy and possible amputation, we were overwhelmed. How were we going to survive being with Joshua in the hospital for 5-6 days every 3 weeks, daily shots while we were home, effects from chemotherapy, plus care for our other children and keep up with cooking, housecleaning, yard work, etc.?

Joshua used to listen to a Christian tape when he was younger that contained a song called "One Step at a Time." One of the lines in the chorus was "I'm climbing my mountain, one step at a time." We realized we needed to apply the wisdom from that song to our lives and focus on one day at a time. If we dwelled on the future, the long hospital stays, possible amputation and uncertainty of survival, it did seem overwhelming!

As we tried to take life one day at a time and trust in God, things became a little more bearable. The doctors and nurses at University of Virginia Children's Medical Center were so helpful and compassionate. The teachers and other staff members tried to make hospital stays more enjoyable with computers, in-house television shows and special programs. Our church and people in the community began to bring meals and help with childcare, cleaning and yard work. A nurse in our church even offered to give Joshua his daily shots, instead of Mom having to give them.

We did survive that ordeal-18 chemo treatments, low blood counts and infections, 5 surgeries including amputation of Joshua's left leg at the hip and feeling sick and fatigued most of the time- with help from God and countless friends. We are grateful to the folks at UVA Children's Medical Center for excellent medical care and to those at Children's Miracle Network for raising funds to support these hospitals. The medical care is outstanding and children's lives are saved thanks to the money donated because of CMN. We have had the privilege of meeting some of the people from CMN and would like to thank them for all their work on behalf of children's hospitals.

Sincerely,

Paul and Linda

Paul and Linda Sundquist

A FUTURE ACTRESS

Enjoys swing dancing, reading, writing, doing crafts and cooking. Her favorite game is to put on a fashion show and do make-overs.

Kathryn Petros

Kathryn's parents became concerned when a pink-eye infection would not heal. Then, when she began to suffer from chronic fatigue and other infections, their concern grew. Kathryn was diagnosed with Acute Lymphocytic Leukemia and was sent to Children's Hospital Los Angeles for her initial therapy but returned to Children's Hospital at Providence (Alaska Medical Center) where she underwent monthly chemotherapy, weekly blood tests, and regular spinal taps.

Now in complete remission, Kathryn is an eighth grade honor student who runs track and plays on the volleyball team. She has been honored as a "Volunteer of the Year" in Alaska for her work with CMN and other charitable organizations. "I CAN do whatever I need to do," says Kathryn. "I had CANcer-not DON'Tcer!"

Kathryn Petros

Dear Andy,

Hi! Thank you so much for letting me be in your book. Being a Children's Miracle Network Champion was an honor, as is being asked to be a part of this book. When I was seven years old, I was diagnosed with Acute Lymphocytic Leukemia. (A.L.L.) My parents and Doctor explained all about my illness to me. Even though I was only seven, I was an active participant in my care, not just a "pin cushion" My family and friends stood by me the whole time. It was a great comfort to know that they were there for me. One thing I learned was that just because a person is handicapped or ill doesn't mean they are weird. All the people I have met in hospitals and clinics have been great.

When I was really sick I was not allowed to go to school, and I was "home schooled". Due to the nature of my cancer, my immune system was not strong enough to fight off even a simple cold. An infection could mean a week long hospital stay, or longer. Chemotherapy made my hair fall out. It has grown back darker, thicker and curlier. It seems a small price to pay to be healthy again.

I would say that having cancer changed my life in many ways. It brought wonderful loving people in my life that worked hard to make me healthy again. It taught compassion and giving to my family in ways we never asked for.

If I had never been sick I would never become involved with helping the hospital during the Children's Miracle Network Telethon. In 1996, I was selected to be the "CMN Champion" from Alaska. That was very exciting. I went to Washington, D.C., and was on the CMN Champions Telethon from Orlando,

Florida. In Florida, I met many people, including CMN co-founder, Marie Osmond. We were in a parade at MGM studios, and at the end of the ride, I got to put my handprints in cement, alongside Miss Osmond's.

Having had cancer has offered me many opportunities and brought me many new friends. Some of my friends tell me I'm lucky because I get to do special things like be on TV, or contribute to books. I don't think anyone would want to have cancer just to have experiences like I have had.

Children's Miracle Network is a great charity. I know that they have helped thousands of children. In Alaska, it has helped to build a new Children's Hospital. The entire pediatrics ward has been remodeled and become the only Children's Hospital in our state. It has become very bright and cheerful and looks a lot friendlier. I was even allowed to be part of the focus groups that helped to pick the themes and designs for the hospital. It was fun!

I would like to thank all the people involved with CMN and at the hospital for their support. CMN provided programs like the Child Life Therapist who helped me face all my procedures and "pokes" without fear. Every time I had Chemo, I would first visit Carol, and we would give her special dolls their own spinal taps, and IV's. It helped to understand what the Doctor had to do for me, to make me better.

When I started second grade, I wrote a short story called, "Chemo is..." and it helped explain what I was going through. My doctors, at Children's in Anchorage and Los Angeles have copies too. Sometimes they are able to share it other kids who have just been diagnosed with cancer. My advice to anyone who is sick like I was, is to learn what they can about their illness. It made it easier for me to share what I was going through to my friends. You don't get cancer for being bad, and you can't catch it from someone. If you feel up to it, keep a journal. Sometimes I just drew happy, sad or sick faces. You can see how you are getting better when you have all happy faces. As of September 1998, I am now "cured" Cancer is now something I had, not that I am living with. I still see my doctor and have to have my blood checked, but pokes don't hurt like they used to!   I guess I have had it easier than other people, even though sometimes it seemed like I had to get "sicker" to get better. So, through spinal taps, bone marrow biopsies, IV's and all the pills I've endured, I did get used to all my treatments, but I am glad it is all over!

Andy, Children's Miracle Network did wonderful things for me, and I am happy to share my story with you. Thanks again for letting me be in your book.

Sincerely,

Kathryn Petros

Kathryn Petros

...ENJOYS GOLFING, SWIMMING AND TEAM ROPING

His favorite TV shows are Hercules and Animorpphs. He enjoys helping out CMN whenever possible.

Rusty Ross

If Rusty could be and do anything he wanted, he would be a hawk and spend his days flying around hunting mice! For now, he is content to enjoy life with his parents and sister, Kara. This is a boy who has maintained a happy disposition and a fun sense of humor despite the challenges he describes in his letter.

Rusty's favorite game is dodge ball, though golf and swimming run a close second. He loves pepperoni pizza, bananas, and the color red. Rusty rides horses quite often with his sister and has recently taught his horse, Spur, to barrel race. He and his family work as volunteers for CMN as often as possible.

Rusty Ross

Dear Andy,

I can't believe that you wanted to hear my story. I am pretty excited, I don't know where to start.

About the last few days of school in 95' I had just turned 9 years old. I was looking forward to playing my first year of peewee baseball. I woke up early one morning, about 2:00, with a sharp pain in my left leg and foot. I could'nt sleep it hurt so bad. My mom put some ice on it and gave me some ibuprofen. I finally got back to sleep for a while but it still hurt pretty bad. When I woke up to get ready for school I couldn't walk on it so I stayed home. Mom and Dad thought it was just growing pains. It was feeling better by the end of the day but was pretty painful when I would put too much weight on it. I went to school the next couple of days but I was limping on it. It was the second to the last day of school and it was hurting a little bit more as the day went on. I went to the school nurse and she noticed that it was starting to swell. She asked me if I wanted to call my mom or stay for the last hour of school. I wanted to stay. When I got home Mom and Dad took me to the doctor. He said it was a real bad infection and sent us up to the hospital right away. I had to get a PIC line put in my arm for antibiotics. Mom had to learn how to give me my medicine through the line. I had to have the line in my arm for about 3 week. The pain had gone way and I was feeling pretty good. I had to be on some pills for a week after I got the PIC line taken out of my arm.

About a week later the pain came back so we went back to the Doctor. He decided to do some tests. I had an MRI the very next morning. We had to wait a day or two for the results of the test. Finally, the Doctor called us to come in to his office. He said he needs to do a biopsy to find out if it is a bone infection or a tumor. It took about a week to get the results from the biopsy. When the results came in everything happened really fast. The doctors told us it was cancerous and that it was Ewings Sarcoma, a fast growing and spreading form of bone cancer. He told us we had to do something right away and there was a chance that I might lose my leg. That scared me but I just wanted the pain to go away. Everything was happening so fast I didn't have time to react. The doctors and my parents told me everything that was going on and what was going to happen if I didn't do everything. Like take all my treatments and medication. From the time I found out that I needed to get started on chemo and the time I actually did was less than a week. I had to have chemo treatments ever three weeks. My Orthopedic doctor explained how he would remove the tumor without amputating my leg. I had to have 5 treatments before I could have the surgery to remove the tumor.

After five treatments of chemo, I had to wait a week to make sure all my counts and everything were back to normal. I was in 11 hours of surgery. They took out the section of my left tibia with the tumor and a little more to make sure they got all the cancer. Then they took the same size section of bone out of my right fibula and grafted it into the place where they removed the tumor. I had to wear a "halo" brace (Ilizarov External Fixator) to hold the bone in place for about six months. The brace had pins going through my bone. I had to have about 3 more surgeries after that one because my bone wasn't healing, they had to put a small plate in my bone to hold it together. I finished all my chemo treatments.

I am now down to six month checkups and everything is still looking really good. No signs of cancer, my leg is healing up just fine and I feel great. I look back and think that it wasn't only hard on me but the rest of the family too. We are all thankful that it is over with and that God must have been watching over us. I wish that everyone's story could end up like mine. Think positive and never give up.

Sincerely,

Rusty Ross

Rusty Ross

"Reality is something you rise above."

– Liza Minneli

POET

...loves to play sports and enjoys reading about the Civil War era. His favorite holiday is Christmas because he gets time to spend with his family.

Chris Wayne

Chris is an active and enthusiastic student at Hastings Senior High School. He is an honor roll student who has lettered in adaptive floor hockey, a state sanctioned sport in Minnesota. Chris is a sport's enthusiast who enjoys downhill skiing and golf. He is working toward a career in sport's broadcasting or public relations.

This young man is a hero to many. His speeches to other people from all walks of life have made him a favorite of companies such as Re/Max and Dairy Queen, as well as the staff at CMN. Chris is a leader. Remember his name. This is a young man who is focused, disciplined, and determined – an unbeatable combination.

Chris Wayne

1900 Meadow View Ct. • Hastings, MN 55033

Mr. Andy Andrews
P. O. Box 3709
Gulf Shores, AL 36547

Dear Andy,

My first goal in life was just to walk. I finally learned to walk when I was 3 years old.
Now at 15, my goals include downhill skiing, playing adaptive floor hockey, and even
playing a round of golf. None of this would even be possible without the doctors and
caring staff at my CMN hospital, Gillette Children's Specialty Healthcare, in St. Paul,
Minnesota.

I was born 3 months premature and weighed 2 pounds 10 ounces at birth. At the age
of about 1 year old, I was diagnosed with cerebral palsy. At the age of 3, I underwent
my first surgery to help me walk better. I have had many other surgeries since and
have 32 incisions from my waist down. Even though there is no cure for cerebral
palsy, these surgeries are done to reduce the spasticity in my leg muscles so I can get
around more efficiently.

Since I have had CP for as long as I can remember, I have had no choice but to
experience the world as a child with a disability. I don't have any regrets about living
with CP for it gives me an unique perspective on life. Two years ago, I wrote a poem
that expressed my feelings about living with a disability.

Silent Whispers-Silent Stares

As I walk down the hall
and hear the silent whispers
and see the silent stares,
It doesn't matter, my mind's not there.

As I walk up the stairs
with people impatiently pushing
from behind,
It doesn't matter, my mind's not there.

At home as I swim in my pool, and wonder
how people can be so cruel,
I think again.
To them it's not cruelty, it's just curiosity.

If they would come up to me
rather than walking away,
or waiting behind,
They would find that my mind is there,
And I'm always willing to share.

Gillette Hospital helps children every day and the Children's Miracle Network helps give Gillette the resources necessary for these miracles to happen. It's great to have an organization like CMN with so many people caring about kids. I have been fortunate to speak on behalf of the Children's Miracle Network and my hospital, both locally and nationally. Through these opportunities, I have been able to meet the people behind the miracles. People who not only give their money but their time and energy to make a difference for kids like me. I am glad to be a voice for children to personally thank everyone involved with CMN.

I believe that everyone has a purpose in life and if you fight through the bad times, the good times will always be waiting. I urge others to make life as good as it can be for themselves and for the other people around them.

Best Wishes,

Chris Wayne

"Making the decision to have a child - it's momentous. It is to decide forever to have your heart go walking around outside your body."

– Elizabeth Stone

Selma

Samson

Their experience has brought them closer and has made them stronger. Samson, is very proud of being the chaplin of the church youth department. Selma, is very proud of being a Christian and having a loving family.

Selma and Samson Davis

On the evening of December 21, 1995, Samson was hit by a van as he stepped off a curb on his way to choir practice. After stabilizing his life threatening injuries, doctors had him flown by helicopter to DeVos Children's Hospital in Grand Rapids, Michigan. There, a team of experts concentrated on reducing the swelling in his brain, which could cause permanent damage or death.

Samson's mother Selma was an obvious participant in this drama and so she agreed to also write a letter for this collection. She is a strong woman with strong faith and is raising a strong son. Incidentally, Samson can now talk and eat normally and shows no signs that he will suffer long term effects of the accident. Samson is once again singing in the choir!

Andy Andrews
P. O. Box 2761
Gulf Shores, AL 36547

Dear Andy,

In December 1995, my brave little son, Samson, entered a battle that changed our lives forever. I was at choir practice when two young boys ran into the church and said a child had just been hit by a van right in front of our church. We all rushed outside. There, in the middle of the street, lay my precious baby boy. He was only 7 years old.

At the hospital, the doctors told me that he had suffered a life-threatening head injury and that he was in a coma. For days, it was touch and go. No one knew if Samson was going to make it. All we could do was pray and wait and pray some more. I'll never forget the sight of him lying there in the hospital bed. He had tubes everywhere. I just wanted to hold him in my arms and hear his sweet voice again.

Then, on Christmas day, right after the Grand Rapids basketball team, the Hoops, came around to visit all the sick children at the hospital, I looked down at Samson and took his tiny hand in mine. Suddenly, those beautiful eyelashes fluttered and he looked up at me! He couldn't walk, talk, or even eat, but Samson was out of the coma. That was our first battle.

Aside from critical head trauma and a broken hand, Samson's jaw was broke in 3 places. Just 2 weeks after they wired his mouth shut, Samson tried to say, "Mama," but he pulled one of the wires loose and swallowed it. They were going to have to do surgery to remove it, but another prayer was answered when he passed it only minutes before being rolled into the operating room. When the doctor went to rewire Samson's jaw, it was completely healed, 4 weeks earlier than they had anticipated!

Samson's battles continued through several hospitals and extensive therapy. Through every obstacle, he never gave up. I was so proud of him. I never left his side and God never left mine. (Whenever you think you don't have anyone, you do!) Cards, gifts, prayers, and friends filled Samson's room through it all. Especially, the support of our wonderful Pastor W.F. Wilson. He visited Samson while in the hospital and made videos of him, which he aired every Sunday on our local TV ministry. This kept the whole town praying for my precious son. Samson recovered miraculously! The doctors were so amazed, that they unanimously voted Samson 'Michigan's Miracle Child of the Year.' His story was in all the newspapers, his face was on the cover of TV Guide, and we received love and support from all over the world. The precious people at Children's Miracle Network sent us to the White House to meet the President and then to Disney World where we met all sorts of stars and sports figures. Samson had the best time! To this day, he still shows all his friends his scrapbook full of all the pictures and autographs he got. As for me, I rejoice in each new day that God gives me with Samson.

…Continued

153

I am so proud of Samson. He has touched so many lives and encouraged other children who were sick or who had special needs. At church, he is the children's chaplain and a real motivator. His prayers are straight from the heart and make the whole congregation want to get up and jump around!

How did we make it through all the battles? With faith the size of a mustard seed. I found out first hand that if you put everything in God's hands, He'll pull you out of every storm life throws you into. Trust God, because His miracles never cease. Samson will be 12 in a few days.

Love from the heart,

Selma Davis

Samson Davis

Andy Andrews
P. O. Box 2761
Gulf Shores, AL 36547

Dear Andy,

When I was 7 years old and on my way to choir practice, a van hit me when I was crossing the street. I didn't see it coming and I guess the driver didn't see me either. Two other kids saw the van hit me and they said it hit me in the ear and I flew up in the air. Mama said I was asleep for a long time before I woke up on Christmas day and she said that was her favorite present.

I had to stay in several different hospitals because I couldn't walk or talk. Since my jaw was broke in so many different places, they had to feed me through a tube. All the doctors and Mama kept calling me their miracle kid because I healed so fast, but it still felt like I was in the hospital a long time. My mom never left me. She went everywhere with me and even helped with my therapy so I could walk and talk and eat by myself. Every time I'd open my eyes, she'd be right there. That made me feel good. The hospital even gave her an apartment next door.

Some people said I wouldn't make it to the year 2000. Every night when I went to sleep in the hospital I would always pray, "Now I lay me down to sleep. I pray the Lord my soul to keep. If I should die before I wake, I pray the Lord my soul to take." Then in the morning when I was still alive, I knew God didn't want me to die yet. Then a bunch of people voted me to be Michigan's Miracle Child since it was a miracle that I could walk and exercise and play again. So they drove us on a bus (that had my picture on it) with other miracle kids from different states and we met President Clinton in the White House. We had to walk a long way and wait for a while because of some secret service stuff and there were big dogs smelling everything. Then we went to Disney World and I met Mary Lou Reton and Steve Young and a bunch of other famous people. Goofy was hanging on Mama the whole time.

I'll be 12 years old on February 13th and I get to wear a tuxedo and go to a special celebration at church. The mayor will be there and I will recite Genesis 1:27 in front of everybody. I still have to do some therapy, but I can play basketball now. I even got to shoot hoops with the Grand Rapids Hoops and I met the Detroit Tigers and got all their autographs.

Kids tease me a lot because I have scars on my face, but I say they can tease me all they want because I made it and I'm still alive. I also tell them, "Don't hang with the bad guys. Hang with God instead." I also pray to God every day and say, "Lord, you see me standing right here and I thank you for another day!"

Sincerely,

Samson Davis

Samson Davis

Lisa and Chase

A DETERMINED AND COURAGEOUS FAMILY

Their difficulties proved that they are a strong family and nothing can stop them. What they have learned has made them accept their difficulties and be prepared to help themselves and others.

Lisa Wilson

When I met Lisa on the phone, I was almost overwhelmed by her sense of purpose. She was calm and yet had a wonderful, light sense of humor about the situation in which her family had found itself.

At the time of our conversation, my wife and I had just been blessed with our first child, a boy, and Lisa's story affected me deeply. My admiration for this family is boundless, and of course, I have an increased level of gratefulness for my own family's situation with a healthy child.

I believe that special people are allowed special situations. By navigating the storms placed in their path, they are granted a grace that brings wisdom and understanding. Lisa, Chase, and the entire Wilson family are without a doubt special people.

Lisa Wilson

Andy Andrews
P. O. Box 2761
Gulf Shores, AL 36547

Dear Andy,

Our family understands the challenges of life's storms more thoroughly than most. We also understand that the chance to write this letter for your book is a part of the opportunity our particular challenge has provided. By touching or inspiring other families, we know that our situation has had a purpose.

Chase was three and a half years old when I took him to the doctor because of an ear infection. He was given an antibiotic for his ear infection and had an allergic reaction to the antibiotic, which caused the tumor to burst, and quickly developed a swollen tummy. Unable to reduce the swelling or find its source, the doctor performed an ultrasound and discovered neuroblastoma. This is a very rare form of cancer in children that originates in the abdomen.

At Children's Hospital in Los Angeles, the specialist who had taken Chase's case, Dr. Seeger, told us that there was no cure for neuroblastoma. There was, however, an experimental protocol that would provide a 10% chance of life. Without treatment, the chances were virtually nonexistent.

Chase's cancer had already progressed to stage four, the final stage, but fortunately, had not gone into any vital organs. We didn't want him to suffer, but decided to go ahead with the experimental treatment, reserving the option to leave the program at any time.

The treatment consisted first of a surgery to remove bone marrow for freezing, followed by six months of extensive chemotherapy which would be five times stronger than that given to an adult. Our three and a half year old would be required to stay at least seven days a month in the hospital. The idea was to get him into remission, then transplant his own bone marrow back into him.

Before chemo, there was an additional operation done to insert a central venous line to the heart and remove the base tumor. Our small ray of hope was jolted the Dr. Seeger told us that they were unable to remove the tumor. It had wrapped itself around the main artery to Chase's heart.

It was Thanksgiving Day when we decided to go ahead with the chemotherapy. It was a long, and quite frankly, horrible experience, but our love and hope and attitude made things bearable. We brought Chase home on Christmas Eve and back to the hospital the day after Christmas. We read stories, played games, and talked. We wanted our son to be normal. We wanted him happy, not depressed.

...Continued

During this time, we had to jealously guard our own attitudes. Many of the other parents we came in contact with allowed the depression to overwhelm everything. We stayed away from these people and their group gatherings. We could not afford the effects of a pity party!

On Easter, we hid eggs in the room while Chase and Amanda, our daughter, closed their eyes. It was a different kind of Easter egg hunt, but we laughed and teased and generally had a great time. My thirtieth birthday was celebrated in the hospital. The doctors and nurses ate cake with us and sang Happy Birthday to me.

Two months after the chemo started, the tumor around the artery was beginning to shrink. Within five months, Chase was in remission. During the sixth month, the doctors did a successful surgery for the removal of all tumors.

Then, the worst time of all hit us. One month later, while waiting for Chase's transplant, the doctors made a startling discovery. The tumors were back. Wes, my husband, and I felt as though someone had taken all the air out of us, but there was nowhere to go but onward, nothing to do but pray.

It was decided to subject Chase to ten straight days of radiation—the last three would be full body radiation—followed by chemotherapy, 24 hours a day, for a full week. We did it.

The next week, in remission, Chase had his bone marrow transplant. For five weeks, he was allowed no body contact from anyone. The family gave blood and platelets many times during this period and gradually; we came to see that the transplant was a success. Even after we went home, Chase had to be very careful. Anytime we went out in public, he had to wear a mask. One afternoon, Chase begged me to take him to a department store near our house. It always hurt me to see people stare at the little boy in the mask so I didn't want to go, but it seemed so important to him.

As we entered the store, he was so excited, running this way and that way. I followed him up one aisle and saw what I was obviously there to buy. It was a picture of Jesus by the Sea of Galilee with children in his lap and spread out around him. Underneath the painting was the inscription, Jesus loves the little children of the world. It still hangs in our home.

...Continued

Chase is now six years out of transplant. He has thyroid problems and cataracts on his eyes. These conditions were caused by the radiation that was instrumental in saving his life. Several skin cancers, from the same source, were also recently removed.

I don't know why our family had to go through this, but I know we are stronger because of it. Chase is still a little boy, but anything he wants to do, he does. He makes straight A's in school and is well prepared for life with a strong will. Our family is closer, better able to deal with everyday challenges that we used to think were a big deal, and we are now able to bring perspective to the lives of some families who might, after reading this letter be glad to have their own problems...and not ours!

Sincerely,

Lisa A. Wilson

Lisa Wilson

FUTURE CONTRACTOR

...he is a very busy young man. But if he had a new hobby it would be snow boarding with his friends. His favorite holiday is Christmas because he loves to open gifts and spend time with his family.

Cory Bacon

Cory wants to be a contractor when he grows up. He will build a home of his own and spend a great deal of time building orphanages in other countries. He has already participated in mission trips with his church. Cory surfs and rides dirt bikes with his brothers, Jesse and Micah. His greatest accomplishment so far is fighting and beating cancer.

Cory and his family have already taken the building blocks of difficulty and are using them to construct an easier future for those who find themselves in similar situations. They work to raise money and awareness for CMN and Ronald McDonald House. A storm in this family's life has created a hunger to provide a safe harbor for others.

CORY BACON

Dear Andy

When I was almost five years old I got stomach aches that got so bad my parents took me to the doctors to see what it was. They took an x-ray and saw a tumor the size of a grapefruit. I remember them saying I had cancer, then sticking a tube in my chest and I was crying alot because I was miserable. Sometimes when I felt good I would ride my I.V. machine down the hall like a skateboard. Once I tipped over the I.V. pole and broke the bottle and cut my leg.

I was sick a lot from the "chemo", but I loved to eat dill pickles and coffee ice cream (but not together)!!! My doctor was really cool , he was real good in encouraging me that I was going to make it.

The fun parts were radiation with "Pee Wee", who acted like Pee Wee Herman; and "Big Foot", Cos was huge who also worked there. Another thing that was fun was going to the Ronald McDonald House, and staying with other kids that were sick like me. And meeting celebrities that would come to visit at the hospital.

I think that having cancer was the worst thing in my life, but after I beat it I got to do so many exciting things like Camp Anuenuu and Camp Ikaika for cancer kids. And I was able to go to Washington D.C. to meet Mrs. Hillary Clinton and I was able to go to Disney World and meet NFL pro football players, along with meeting Amy Grant. All this great stuff was possible through the Chilrens Miracle Network. I was chosen by them to represent the Hawaiian Islands. I don't recommend having cancer, so if you smoke.....put out that cancer stick!!!!

I heard God tell me I was going to make it, and He knew I had a longer life to live. I give Him credit for healing me and my doctors and nurses for helping God with my treatments.

The End

Cory Bacon

Cory Bacon

FUTURE PHYSICAL THERAPIST

...would like to turn back time and live in the 1920's. She enjoys the dress, music and dance of that era.

Keishandria Humphreys

Keishandria has experienced a radical change in her life's direction. Because of the challenge posed by a normally simple illness, she has turned her thoughts toward others. Keke, as she is known to her family and friends, has developed an intense desire to study physical therapy.

Keke is eighteen years old and will soon be studying at the University of Tennessee at Chattanooga. She is very good at sports, especially basketball, and loves to read and work with her computer. She counts as her proudest achievement the victory over her illness. Now, she understands, will come a struggle to help other children in similar situations.

KeKe Humphreys

Andy Andrews
P.O. Box 2761
Gulf Shores, Alabama 36547

Dear Andy,

What a great honor to be able to put my story in your book. I have been asked to write my story of being a miracle child. I have been so blessed to have that title. I first must give my thanks to God my savior Jesus Christ. Without them there would be no me. I would like to also thank the doctors and nurses at LeBonheur Children's Hospital in Memphis ,TN. I am most thankful for them they made me feel like my 3 and a half month stay at the hospital was like a home away from home.

The story behind this miracle starts with a simple case of strepthroat which turned bad. I wasn't feeling well and my mom took me to my pediatrician he diagnosed me with strep. He gave me the usually medicine and sent me home. I took the medicine but I didn't get any better. My mom took me back to the doctor and they rushed me to the hospital. My blood pressure was dropping and they started IV's as soon as I got there. From that point on I do not remember up until around February 16 a few days after Valentine's day. The day I went into the hospital was January 13. While in the Hospital I had a number if IV's 26 to be exact. I had to be put on a heart monitor and a respirator. I also had a tractomony because of the internal bleeding the tube in my throat caused. My kidneys soon failed and I was put on a dialysis. I had a number of blood transfusions. After all I went through I also had some liver failure. I went through a lot in that hospital. I had to go through extensive rehabilitation at a local rehab hospital. I had to learn how to walk and build my strength up to do the basic skills to get through my everyday life.

It was a long haul but I made it through on top. I don't think I would have made it without the help of God. I would also like to thank all of my family and friends because with their support and prays I would have never made it through this horrible situation. I need to also make a special thanks to all of the wonderful doctors and nurse at the hospital.   Once again thank you Andy for this wonderful privilege to tell my story and the wonderful people who helped me through it. Now I'm all well and will be starting college this fall at the University of Tennessee at Chattanooga. I will be studying to be a physical therapist.

Thanks

Keishandria Humphreys

"Never doubt that a small group of thoughtful, committed people can change the world. Indeed, it is the only thing that ever has."

– Margaret Mead

FUTURE PILOT

...enjoys life to the fullest and would like to be a bird and spend the entire day enjoying the beautiful freedom of flight.

David Pierson

As soon as David is able, he will be getting his pilot's license in order to fly all over the world. I, for one, have no doubt that David will make this dream come true. The accident that he had forced him to learn a focus he may not have been aware he possessed. David focused through surgeries, rehab, and recovery and has now become a grateful and confident young man.

David has not lost his sense of adventure. He enjoys football, soccer, track, and would one day like to take up rock climbing. David is also a pretty funny guy. He told me that his dad is an attorney, but that his mom has the hardest job in the world. He says, "She cooks, cleans, and takes care of a family while trying to stay sane!

DAVID PIERSON

Andy Andrews
P.O. Box 3709
Gulf Shores, Alabama 36547

Dear Andy,

   Thank you for asking me to contribute the details of my personal experience on overcoming obstacles that I have faced. I feel greatly honored.

   July 6th, 1996 truly opened my eyes to the delicate beauty of life. On that fateful day, I was in a horrible ATV accident in which I sustained an immense impact that shattered my facial and cranial bones. My bottom lip was torn, exposing bare gums where teeth once set, and I bled from my mouth, nose, knees, and back. It was a rather excruciating experience with surprisingly positive results.

   It took several months and about a thousand balloons and get-well cards to fully recover from that devastating accident. Since then, I have undergone four separate surgeries to literally rebuild my face and correct problems with my teeth and eyes, and each time relatives and friends have showered me with love and concern.

   It has been a little over two years since my accident, and I still have somewhat mixed feelings about it. I wish that I had never experienced the pain and my family the anguish, but, at the same time, I am glad that I had the accident. It has provided me with a clarity and understanding of the beauty of life that, had I not crashed, my eyes would never see. I realize, now more than ever, that life is an indescribably precious gift that I have to cherish and to fulfill. Being so close to losing that gift has brought me a clearer understanding of my responsibilities and has helped me to love myself and others unconditionally.

   I am forever indebted to the many wonderful doctors that helped me and to Children's Miracle Network for helping Children's Hospitals all over the country provide the same unparalleled love and care that I received.

                                        Thanks again,

                                        David Pierson
                                        David Pierson

Enjoys all types of sports and plays like a winner. His attitude is to be the best and his outlook toward life is always positive.

Ryan Dawson

At the age of fourteen, Ryan's focus in life changed dramatically. His hope to become an NBA basketball star was replaced by the desire to keep his leg. What seemed to be a simple injury was actually the beginning of chemotherapy and surgery to combat bone cancer. Faced with the possibility of losing his leg, Ryan underwent a limb-saving operation to replace cancerous bone with healthy donor bone. Ryan now walks without crutches.

Ryan loves sports and continues to display a positive attitude toward life. He says that before the operation, he wanted to be like Michael Jordan. Now he's decided to be like Tiger Woods. But that could change, too. Having spent so much time at Children's Hospital, Ryan has now expressed an interest in pursuing a career as a physician.

RYAN DAWSON

Dear Andy,

I appreciate the opportunity to share my story with you and others. I hope it will be helpful to others who may go through a similar situation.

In December of 1996, I was 13 years old, going to school, and like most 13 year old boys, very active in sports. At the time, I was playing basketball and began having problems with my right leg. We noticed a small knot just below my right knee. Even though my family thought it was just one of those normal bumps that boys get while playing rough during contact sports, we decided to have it checked. We saw a few doctors before having a MRI done on January 3rd, 1997. From there, it was x-rays, scans, and finally a biopsy on January 10th that confirmed that I had a malignant Ewings Sarcoma tumor. I was so scared. When they told me I had cancer, the first thing that came to my mind was if I was going to die. We began chemotherapy, also called "chemo", immediately after the biopsy. The plan was to have three months of chemo, a major surgery, and then finish the chemo the next 9 months.

The chemo had a positive affect on the tumor. The major surgery that took place in April of '97, involved removing a five-inch piece of my fibula, replacing it with a donor bone, and removing a large area of tissue. It was a very successful surgery. Today, almost 2 years after the surgery and over a year since my last chemo treatment, I am "cancer free."

I've learned a lot from my illness. First, the importance of faith, family, friends, and attitude. The prayers and support of everyone we know, and some we don't, were very important also. Second, just how fragile life really is for all of us. All of the little kids in the children's ward made me feel pretty guilty. I may think I have it bad, but when I see little 2-year olds hooked up to monitors, it makes me feel sorry for them because I know that they don't really understand. It's important to do something special for someone in need whenever the opportunity exist. The Children's Miracle Network is a prime example of tireless and dedicated people working together to help kids and their families who are in need of it. We plan to help them in any way that we can.

My illness has made me a much stronger, but caring person. I look at and approach things differently. For those facing, or in the future, may face a similar life-threatening illness, I would say: <u>never, ever</u> allow a negative thought to enter your mind by always maintaining a positive attitude and thinking positive thoughts. I always say "Put humor in everything you do." In any situation, you can always find something to laugh or smile about. Remember: laughter is contagious.

Sincerely,

Ryan Dawson

Children's Miracle Network is an international non-profit organization dedicated to raising funds for and awareness of children's hospitals. Begun in 1983, CMN's first fund-raising effort was a television special broadcast by 30 television stations and originating from a small studio in Provo, Utah. That first year CMN and 22 hospitals in the United States raised $4.7 million.

Now CMN produces the largest television fund raiser in the world. From 1987 until 1995, the annual 21-hour international television special originated live from Disneyland. In 1996 CMN again took up the mantle of leadership and moved its annual broadcast to Walt Disney World and an exciting sports format. The fund raising campaign and broadcast, both called CMN Champions, now benefit 170 children's hospitals. CMN Champions airs over a caring network of 200 television stations in the United States, Canada and Mexico, and annually benefits 14 million children suffering from every affliction. In 17 years, CMN has raised more than $1.2 billion for children's hospitals, $192 million in 1999 alone.

CMN's founding pledge, to keep 100 percent of donations in the area in which they were raised and to put children first in all it does, remains at the core of its philosophy. CMN, however, is not the same organization it was in 1983. Each year thousands of special events are organized and executed under the CMN Champions umbrella in communities large and small across North America.

Why Champions? A champion is someone who has won victory. No word better describes what the 14 million children treated in CMN-affiliated hospitals each year have accomplished. But no victory is won alone. Doctors, nurses and therapists provide care and treatment. Families provide love and hope. Donors at every level make possible charity care and vital equipment purchases. Each of these groups, and many more, championed these children and helped them win life's greatest battles.

Many major corporations and associations feature CMN Champions in their marketing plans. It's a way of doing well by doing good. In teaming up with CMN Champions, a company helps children, increases its public exposure and positively affects the bottom line. Moreover, CMN Champions has redefined the traditional television fund raiser. New and exciting programming under the banner of CMN Champions attracts the entire sporting world to the cause of children. CMN Champions showcases individual programs like IOF Foresters Champions Across America and Canada and the CMN Champions Celebrity Golf Challenge.

In 17 years, Children's Miracle Network has evolved into the dominant organization actively providing better health care for millions of children through its affiliated hospitals. The 170 children's hospitals associated with CMN represent the premier facilities in their respective communities, and some of the finest hospitals in the world.

Of course the television special remains the largest CMN Champions event of the year. By tradition, the program takes place the first weekend following the U.S. Memorial Day holiday. Each year, CMN Champions will feature sports and entertainment personalities in educational, entertaining and informative programming.

Children's Miracle Network
4525 South 2300 East, Suite 202 • Salt Lake City, Utah 84117
(801) 278-8900 • FAX (801) 277-8787
www.cmn.org

Alphabetical Index

For booking information,
additional copies of this series,
or to see other popular items by Andy Andrews
such as comedy cassettes, motivational tapes
and a variety of t-shirts, please call
for a free color brochure

1-800-726-ANDY
24 hours a day

or you may write to:

Andy Andrews
P.O. Box 17321
Nashville, TN 37217

USA

or

Visit Andy's Web Site At:

www.AndyAndrews.com